Runes

Learning Guide for Reading Runes

*(Learn the Realms of Runes Divination and Magic
From a-z+ Tips and Tricks)*

Jeffery Taylor

Published By **Ryan Princeton**

Jeffery Taylor

Runes: Learning Guide for Reading Runes (Learn the Realms of Runes Divination and Magic From a-z+ Tips and Tricks)

ISBN   978-1-998769-20-9

No part of this guidebook shall be reproduced in any form without permission in writing from the publisher except in the case of brief quotations embodied in critical articles or reviews.

Legal & Disclaimer

Table Of Contents

Chapter 1: The Players 1

Chapter 2: Yggdrasil And The Nine Worlds
.... 17

Chapter 3: The Master Builder 52

Chapter 4: The Children Of Loki 81

Chapter 5: Freya's Unique Wedding..... 104

Chapter 6: What Happened To The Runes
And How Runes Came Into Existence... 128

Chapter 7: The Elder Futhark 152

Chapter 8: What The Runes Can Be Used
To Help With Magic And Divination 174

Chapter 1: The Players

Within Norse mythology, a variety of gods and goddesses have been referred to as. Within these stories, we'll find numerous of them. The majority of stories include two gods, Odin as well as his son Thor as well as Odin's blood brother Loki the giant's son who is a part of his father, the Aesir within Asgard.

Odin is one of the gods of the Norse god.

Odin is the most powerful and the oldest god.

Odin is a keeper of an array of secrets. Odin was blessed with a sharp sense of knowledge. Beyond that it was that he sacrificed himself to learn about the runes and to gain strength.

He was suspended from Yggdrasil the world tree for nine days. The tip of a spear struck his hand, seriously damaging the man. The wind was a thumping force as they whipped his frame around. He didn't eat , drink or eat anything for the next nine days or nights. He was alone and in pain with the light of his life becoming dim.

When the sacrifice of his was a dark fruits He was cold, suffering and was on the brink of death. In the bliss of his agony He looked around, and the runes came out to him. He was well-versed in the runes and knew their power. The rope broke, and he shouted and fell off the tree.

He was finally able to grasp the notion of magic. He now had control of the whole universe.

Many names are known as Odin. Odin is the all-father, the god of the dead and god of the Gallows. He is also the god of freight, and the god of prisoners. He has a distinct name (for it is believed that he worships in many forms and languages, however it is always Odin that they worship).

He hides himself and travels from place to place to view the world as others observe it.

He is tall with the cloak and a hat.

Two ravens are that are named Huginn and Muninn which are the words for "think" as well as "memory," respectively. These birds travel between the globe, seeking out news stories and providing Odin any details. They sit on Odin's shoulders and whisper some words into his ears.

As he sits on his throne high at Hlidskjalf the throne, he is watching every single thing, regardless of the location. He will not let anything go unnoticed.

He brought war to the world. Battles begin with the throwing of a spear into the enemy army, committing the battle and the loss to Odin. If you are able to survive a war the reason is Odin's mercy, but if you lose, it's because of his treachery.

If you lose your courage during battle In the event of your death, the Valkyries lovely battle maidens, who collect the souls of great dead will transport your body to Valhalla. They will greet you in Valhalla in which you can be able to drink, fight, feast and fight under the guidance of Odin.

Thor's

Thor's thunderer was Odin's father Thor. Thor is honest, whereas Odin's father Odin is fraudulent, and he's kind, while his father is shrewd.

He is huge Red-bearded, imposing, and powerful and by far the strongest of gods. The strength belt he wears enhances his strength When it is worn his strength increases by two times.

Thor's weapons are Mjollnir the hammer of Thor, which is awe-inspiring created by dwarfs for him. If you look at Mjollnir and you learn the tale, the ice giants, trolls mountains giants, and trolls shudder because it has killed so many of their companions and brothers. Thor wears iron gloves to hold the grip of his Hammer.

Jord the goddess of earth was Thor's mother. Modi and Magni, the furious and Magni the powerful are Thor's sons. Thrud Thor, the strong Thor's daughter.

The name of his wife is Sif, and she is a brunette with golden hair. Before she got married to Thor they had children called Ullr and Thor is Ullr's stepfather. Ullr is a god of hunting who hunts using bows and arrows, and is also god of skiing.

Thor is Midgard's and Asgard's guardian.

There are many stories concerning Thor and his adventures. You'll find a few of these here.

Loki is an imaginary character.

Loki is stunning. He's convincing, plausible and likable. He is probably the most cunning subtle, astute, and delicate out of the Asgardians. It's unfortunate, however that he carries many dark thoughts within him, lots of hatred, envy and lust.

Loki was the child of Laufey who was called Nal or needle due to her slim beautiful, striking, and sharp appearance. Farbauti, the giant was believed as his dad. his name translates to "he who strikes with deadly force," and Farbauti was not as dangerous as his name implied.

Loki can be seen flying through the skies with his shoes that fly and he is able to alter his appearance to appear like animals or other humans However, his most powerful weapon lies in his brain. Loki is more clever, clever, and deceitful than all gods or giants. Even Odin isn't as clever as Loki.

Loki was Odin's birth twin. The gods of the other gods aren't sure what happened to him or how Loki was introduced to Asgard. He is Thor's friend as well as his sworn enemy. The gods are tolerant of him, perhaps due to his schemes and plans help them, even as they cause them to be in trouble.

Loki can make the world more exciting, but also makes it less secure. Loki is the god of cleverness and the godfather of monsters, and the creator of all the woes.

Loki drink a lot of alcohol and, when he drinks it is difficult to control his emotions, vocabulary and behavior. Loki and his family will be in attendance at Ragnarok the day that marks the end of the world, but they won't fight with the Asgardian gods.

BEFORE THE ENTRY and BEFORE AND

There was nothing prior to the beginning of time--no planets, stars or stars--just the misty world that was void of form and shape and the fire-world was never slowed down.

Niflheim The dark world, Niflheim lies towards the north. Eleven poisonous rivers cut through the mist of the area, each coming from the same source that was at the center of all this, the massive raging storm called Hvergelmir. Niflheim was extremely cold, and the hazy fog that covered everything was hanging in thick. Smoke obscured the clouds as well as the floor was surrounded with chilly fog.

Muspell was located to the south. Muspell had a massive flame. Every room in the room lit up and ignited. Muspell was bright, and Niflheim is dark dark, molten, and the misty world was made of ice. The land was submerged in the intense flames of a blacksmith's furnace There was nothing solid, no sky. There were only sparks and glowing fire, molten rock and smoldering embers.

Surtr the god of the night, who lived among the gods, was standing near an edge to the fire in the middle of the mist, where it burns to light, and the land is sunk in Muspell. He is standing right now. He is wielding the fiery sword while the bubbling hot lava as well as the icy mist look exactly the same for him.

It is believed that Surtr will depart from his position only at Ragnarok at the end in the universe. Surtr will rise from Muspell with his sword of ablaze and take over the Earth by igniting fire. the gods will be destroyed one by one in front of Surtr.

II

There was a space in between Muspell and Niflheim It was a hollow area that was empty and void of form. The mist's rivers were able to flow into the void, known by the name of Ginnungagap which is also called"the "yawning gaps." The poisoned rivers slowly consolidated into huge glaciers in the space between mist and fire during a period of time. The ice on the north area of the gap covered by a haze of frozen fog and hail particles and hail, while towards the south, where glaciers met with the land of fire the embers and sparks of Muspell's were able to penetrate the ice, and the warm breezes emanating from the flames created the air above the glaciers as supple and pleasant as a spring-like day.

The ice was melting when it came into contact with the fire and life emerged from the water that was melting and the resemblance of humans that were bigger than the universe and more important than any other giant there could be or ever have been. It wasn't female or male however it was simultaneously.

The beast, also known as Ymir was the first giant to be born.

Ymir isn't the only thing who emerged from melted ice: There was also an cow without horns that was more important than our imagination could ever contain. To eat and drink she took a bite of frozen ice chunks that were salty while the milk she came out through her four cow udders gushed like rivers. The milk was nourishing Ymir.

Milk caused the gigantic to expand.

Audhumla was the name given to the cow According to Ymir.

The cow's pink tongue took people off the ice blocks. The first day, just hairs of a man were revealed on the second day his head, and on the 3rd day the body of a man as a whole was revealed.

This was Buri God's main ancestor.

Ymir was asleep, and during the time it was asleep it had a baby. both female and male giant beneath Ymir's left arm along with the six-headed giant that was born from its legs. All giants are descendents of the children of Ymir.

Buri got married to one of the giants, and had a son who they called Bor. Bor was married to Bestla the daughter of the giant They had 3 sons: Odin, Vili, and Ve.

Three sons of Bor's, Odin, Vili, and Ve who grew into men. The three brothers could have seen the blazes from Muspell along with the dark of Niflheim from the distance as they grew however, they were aware that each was going to be killed. The brothers remained lost in Ginnungagap the vast chasm between mist and fire. They may have been somewhere.

There was no ocean, sand, grass , trees, rocks, dirt moon, stars, or even the moon. In the past there was no the universe, no heaven and there was no earth. The empty space was not to be found. It was just a blank space waiting to be full of life and nature.

It was the time to begin creating all of it. Ve, Vili, and Odin shared glances and debated the things to be accomplished in the absence of Ginnungagap. They discussed the universe as well as life and the future.

Odin, Vili, and Ve defeated the gigantic Ymir. It was inevitable. There was no other choice for establishing the universes. It was the first step in all things, and the end of everything which allowed living things to come into existence.

They struck the massive beast with their slashes. Blood gushed out in staggering amounts from Ymir's body and blood fountains that were as salty as seawater and as dark as oceans gushed out in a flood that was so intense, sudden and massive that it washed away and submerged all the gigantic beasts. (Only Bergelmir, Ymir's grandson and his wife, escaped by climbing up on a wooden box which carried them as an old boat. They are the ancestors of the giants that we see and fear today.)

Odin along with his brother fashioned the soil using the bone of Ymir. They put the bones of Ymir in cliffs, mountains.

Our pebbles and rocks, and the sand and gravel that you see, are Ymir's teeth and bone fragments broke into pieces in the hands of Odin, Vili, and Ve in their battle against Ymir.

The oceans that covered the globe were the result of Ymir's sweat and blood.

If you look up in the sky to view the inner workings of Ymir's head. The stars that you see at night and the planets, the shooting stars, and comets are the fires that shot from the Muspell fires. What about the cloud formations that you see in the daytime? They were once the brains of Ymir and who knows what they're thinking today.

III

It is believed that the Earth has a flat disc with oceans surrounding it. Giants reside on the edges of the country, close to the deepest oceans.

To keep the giants back, Odin, Vili, and Ve created a wall of Ymir's eyelashes. They put it in the earth's middle. Midgard is the title that was given to the region within the wall.

Midgard was empty. There was no one who walked the meadows, or fished in the green waters. No one ventured into the rocky mountains or gazed at the sky.

Odin, Vili, and Ve realized that a planet can't be an actual world unless it's been or is currently occupied. They looked high and low for people , but came up empty handed.

Then, on the rocky shingle near the edge of the ocean they found two sea-tossed logs which were floating there on the tides, and were swept into the sea.

First logs were ash log. Ash trees are tough and gorgeous, with roots that are deep. Its wood is simple to cut and will not break or break. Ashwood is perfect for spear handles and tool shafts.

The other log they came across close to the first on the sand and identical to the one they were nearly touching it was an elmwood wood log. Elm trees are graceful and its wood is strong enough to be used to create the most durable beams and planks as well as to create a stunning home or hall.

The gods gathered two logs. They set them in the sand until they were about the identical height of humans. Odin took them in and kissed them, breathing life, one by one. They weren't dead, rotting logs on the beach. They were living.

Vili has given them the determination, intelligence and motivation. They could now transfer to another institution and would like to do so.

Ve cut the logs. Then he gave them the form like people. Then he cut off their ears, so they could hear, their eyes so that they could see, as well as their lips to allow them to speak.

Two naked people sat on two logs on sand. Ve had cut one with male genitals while the other had female Genitals.

In the freezing sea-spray that dripped off the beach on the edge of the planet, three brothers made clothing for the female and the man to protect their bodies and keep warm.

Then, they identified the two characters they had made: Ask, the man or Ash Tree and Embla The woman or Elm.

Ask to be a part of the family, as well Embla was the mother and father of us all each human being owes his existence to its parents, who then have a responsibility to them, and they then are owed their life to the parents of their children, and who then have a responsibility to the parents of their children and all the way to.

If you travel long enough back in time, everyone is a descendent of Ask as well as Embla as our ancestors. Embla and Ask kept their place in Midgard in peace in the wall made of Ymir's eyelashes, a gift from the gods. They'll make their home in Midgard and be safe from monsters and giants as well as all the dangers that lurk in the desert. They could raise their kids peacefully in Midgard.

This is the reason Odin is often referred to as the Allfather. Since he was god's father and Odin breathed life into our grandparents grandparents grandparents. Odin is the one who created everyone of us, regardless of whether we're mortals or gods.

Chapter 2: Yggdrasil And The Nine Worlds

Ash tree is one type of tree that is found in the United the mighty Ash trees Yggdrasil is among the most beautiful and impressive of all trees, and also the highest. It is spread across nine worlds and joins them all. It is the biggest and most stunning of every tree. The roots of this tree reach up to the sky.

It's so large that the ash's root is distributed across three continents and three wells provide it with water.

The very first and most significant source is the one that leads towards the dark side, Niflheim which is the place which existed prior to all other locations. Hvergelmir is the constantly churning source located in deep in the dark realm is so loud it can be heard as an roaring kettle. Nidhogg, the dragon that is a part of the oceans, is always gnawing at the bottom from beneath.

The second one connects to Mimir's well located situated in the land of the giants of the frost.

There is an eagle that sits between the eyes of an eagle and watches the top of the world tree having a vast knowledge of the world tree.

Ratatosk is a squirrel who lives among the trees of the world. Tree's It transmits news and messages from Nidhogg the terrifying corpse-eater the eagle back. The squirrel plays tricks on both and is a frightened delight, provoking anger.

Four stags roam around the huge tree's roots devouring the bark and leaves. There's a large number of snakes near the tree's bottom, chewing off the root.

The possibility exists to climb to the top of the tree. Odin was hung in the sacrifice of this oak, transforming this world-tree into a Gallows, and himself into the god of the gallows.

The gods don't attempt to climb the trees of the universe. They make use of Bifrost which is the bridge that crosses the rainbow that allows them to travel across the world. Only gods could traverse the rainbow. Any giants of ice or trolls trying to climb up it to get into Asgard will be burnt.

The nine realms of

The Aesir's home is Asgard. Odin is known as this house his home. Alfheim is home to the light Elf. Stars and sun are equally magnificent as the light elves.

Dwarves (also called dark Elves) reside beneath the mountains and create their own creations in Nidavellir which is also called Svartalfheim.

Midgard is the home of men and women, and it's here that we call home.

Jotunheim is the home of the frost giants as well as mountain giants. Here they wander, live and are surrounded by halls.

Vanaheim is where you can find Vanaheim is the home of Vanir. There are many Vanir gods are found in Asgard along with the Aesir and the Aesir as well as Vanir. Vanir are gods united through peace agreements.

The dark, misty realm of Niflheim.

Surtr awaits you in Muspell the land of fire.

There's as well Hel which is a city named after the king of it and where those who did not die bravely in battle are buried.

The final roots of the global tree takes you to the spring in Asgard which is the home of the gods where the Aesir reside. The gods gather here each day to discuss their councils and it's where that they'll gather in the last times of this world prior to the final fight of Ragnarok. Urd's Well is what is known as.

The Norns are three wise maidens that have three sisters. They care for the well and make sure that the roots of Yggdrasil are cleaned and taken care of. Urd is the one who owns the well. she is destiny and fate. Urd is part of your history. Verdandi is a name that refers to "becoming," and whose domain is in the present, and Skuld who's name is "that that is destined," and whose domain is the future, are in her.

Your life will be determined in the hands of the Norns. There are other Norns in addition to the three Norns. There are gigantic horns and the elf Norns and tiny Norns as well as Vanir Norns Good Norns and poor norns and they decide your fate. Some words give us great lives, while some give us complicated, short or devious lives. They determine what you will become such as giant horns and elf Norns and tiny Norns as well as Vanir Norns and good Norns and poor Norns. Some words provide us with good lives While others provide us with complicated, short or demented lives. They determine your destiny and will be at Urd's well.

MIMIR'S HEAD, the EYE OF ODIN

Mimir's well is situated in Jotunheim where live the giants. It rises out of the depths into the Earth and is fed by Yggdrasil which is the tree of all time. Mimir The wise and wisest of the memory's keepers is well-versed on many areas. The source of his wisdom is and he would take a drink every morning when the world was still young by dipping his Gjallarhorn into the water and then draining it.

In the past, long in the past, when the worlds were still young Odin put on his long cape and cloak and set out across the land of the giants, taking risks to attain Mimir who was the source of wisdom.

"One drink from the well water in your home, Uncle Mimir," Odin stated. "All I need is."

With a shaking of his head, Mimir expressed his disappointment with the current situation. Mimir is the sole person that drank from the fountain. He was silent. Those who are silent tend to commit mistakes.

Odin said, "I am your nephew." "Bestla My mother was also your mother." "That does not suffice." Mimir said emphatically.

"I'll enjoy one drink. I'll be smart if consume my drink from your fountain, Mimir. "Set the price."

Mimir stated, "Your eye is my price." "You've been eyeing me in the water."

Odin did not ask about whether he was actually laughing. The trek to the well of Mimir had been long and difficult, since they had traveled across vast expanses of terrain. Odin was capable of putting his life in danger in order to reach his destination. He was in a position to go far and beyond to obtain the wisdom he wanted.

Odin's expression was written.

He said, "Give me a knife."

He carefully placed his eyes into the water after completing his work. Through the water it was looking at Odin. Odin took a drink from the Gjallarhorn that he put up towards his mouth after filling it up with the water that was in Mimir's bathtub. The water was frozen. He consumed it all. He was swollen with wisdom. With just one eye, he could see further and more clearly than with two eyes.

Following that, Odin was given new names: Blind, the blind King, Hoare, the one-eyed god and Baleyg the god of flaming eyes.

Odin's eye is preserved Mimir's well, which is surrounded by water that supply the planet with Ash, and is capable of seeing anything.

The time dragged on. Odin was sent Mimir into the Vanir in the role of an adviser to Hoenir, the Aesir god Hoenir who would become the new head of the Vanir as the conflict among the Aesir as well as the Vanir was about to come to an end. The two were trading chiefs and warriors.

Hoenir was handsome and tall and was the look of the King. Hoenir spoke like a king and made smart decisions when Mimir was present to advise him. But in the absence of Mimir wasn't present, Hoenir seemed unable to make a decision his own fate, and the Vanir became exhausted. They retaliated against

Mimir instead of Hoenir by cutting off the head of Mimir and the head to Odin.

Odin was not angry at all. He applied some herbs to Mimir's scalp to keep the head from becoming rotten and whispered incantations and charms to it as he did not wish for Mimir's wisdom to be lost. Mimir finally opened his eyes and began speaking to him. Mimir's advice was spot-on like it has always been.

Odin brought Mimir's body back to the deep beneath the world tree, where he placed the head in front of his eyes and gazed into the waters of experience and future.

Heimdall, god's watchman, was gifted Gjallerhorn from Odin. The gods will be awakened upon the day that the Gjallarhorn is blowing regardless of the location or how deep they sleep.

Heimdall will only blast the Gjallerhorn only once, during Ragnarok in the middle of the film.

The TREASURES OF GOD

Sif was Thor's gorgeous wife. She was a member of the Aesir. Thor loved her for who she was in addition to her fair skin and blue eyes with red lips, a beautiful smile, and her hair, which was the shade of a field in summer barley.

Thor awakeed and looked at Sif who was asleep. The beard of his was scrabbled. He then tapped his wife's shoulder with a large , heavy hand. He asked, "What happened to you?"

Her eyes were the hue of summer skies when she opened her eyes. "What do you mean by that?" she asked while her head moved in a tangled manner. Her fingers reached out to her pink hair as she gently layed it down trying to test it. She was shocked when she gazed at Thor.

She declared, "My hair."

Thor smiled and smiled and nodded. He declared, "It's gone." "He's removed you of the hair." "He?" Sif asked.

Thor did not speak. Then he put on his belt of power, Megingjord that amplified his enormous strength. He declared, "Loki." "Loki is the person who was responsible for it."

"Why did you think this?" Sif was asked, while frantically moving her hair as if the gentle flutter of her fingers could make her hair grow back.

"Because," Thor explained, "when something goes wrong my first thought is Loki. It saves you lots of time."

Thor realized that Loki's doors were shut, so he ran through it, smashing the door. Thor took Loki into his arms and just demanded, "Why?"

"Why?" you might be asking yourself. Loki had a completely innocent look that he displayed on his face.

"It's Sif's hair. The golden kid in my life is wife. It was breathtaking. What made you decide to cut it off?"

The face of Loki was mix of emotions, including cunning deceit, confusion and truculence. Thor offered Loki an enthusiastic shake. Loki lowers his head, pretending to be ashamed. "It was funny. "I was drunk."

Thor's forehead was furrowed. "Sif's hairline was the greatest accomplishment. Many would think she was punished for shaving her head. She committed a crime she shouldn't have been doing with people she shouldn't have been doing it with."

"Indeed, indeed. This is the truth," Loki said. "I'm sure that they'll be thinking the same thing. Unfortunately, as I took her hair out of the root, she'll be completely bald for the duration all of life...

"No She won't," Thor said, his face shaking when he looked up at Loki He was now lifting over his head.

"I'm worried she'll do it," I say. Scarves and hats, however are always in stock. ."

"She will not go hairless for the rest of her existence," Thor predicted. "Because Loki's son, I'm going fracture every bone inside your body if don't get her hair back immediately.

Every single one. I'll go back and smash every bone within your body if the hair doesn't develop in a proper way. And again. I'll be able to master doing it if I practice it daily," he said, looking a little more positive.

Loki shouted, "No!" "I haven't been able to restore her hair to its the right place. It's not how it works." "It could take me around one hour break each bone within your body today," Thor speculated. However, with a bit of the practice, I'm sure that I can cut it down to around fifteen minutes. It'll be exciting to watch the results." He started to break the first bone.

Loki shrieked, "Dwarfs!"

"Excuse me?"

"Dwarves!" The narrator exclaims. They could make something. They could offer Sif gold hair and hair that binds to her scalp, and grow gorgeous natural golden hair. They'd be able to accomplish this. They could believe me when I say."

"Then you'll need to and talk with the people," Thor advised. Then he then threw Loki down from a high point.

Before Thor could even break any bone, Loki scrambled to his feet and bolted away.

He put on shoes that would allow him to fly in the air and travelled to Svartalfheim in the area where the workshop of the dwarfs are situated. The three dwarfs are referred to as the children of Ivaldi He decided that they were the most imaginative artisans of all.

Loki was underground at their forge. "Hello, Ivaldi's sons. "I inquired around, and everyone here agrees that Brokk as well as his younger brother Eitri they are among the most skilled dwarf craftsmen or ever have been," Loki said.

"No," one of Ivaldi's sons responded. "It's ours," says the narrator. We are among the best artisans in the world.

"I am confident I am certain Brokk as well as Eitri will come up with masterpieces as great than yours."

The youngest of Ivaldi's sons declared, "Lies!" "I don't trust on those incompetents who are clumsy to shoe the horse."

The shrewdest and youngest of Ivaldi's sons shook their heads. "Whatever they think of is something we can make better."

Loki told Loki, "I hear they've questioned you." "There there are 3 treasures. The Aesir gods will determine who is the most valuable treasure. Hair, in fact is among the precious stones you own. "Perfect shiny hair with golden highlights that will never stop growing."

"We are able to achieve this," one of Ivaldi's sons told him. They were so similar , even Loki couldn't tell the difference.

Loki went up the mountain to meet Brokk the dwarf who was in the same workshop as the brother Eitri. "Ivaldi's sons are making three treasures to give to gods in Asgard," Loki explained. "The treasures will be evaluated to be a gift from the gods. The sons of Ivaldi want me to inform you that they're certain that you as well as your brother Eitri are not capable of producing anything as impressive as what they have. You've been called 'fumble-fingered and ignorants.'"

Brokk was not an acrobatic one-handed knucklehead. He stated, "This looks incredibly fishy to me, Loki." "Are you certain that this isn't the fault of you?" It's the kind of thing you'd want to do, creating tension in between Eitri and me, and Ivaldi's kids."

Loki appeared to be as authentic as he could, which was shockingly unassuming. He said in a casual manner "Nothing about me." "I thought you ought to take note of this."

"And are you personally involved to this?" Brokk was curious.

"Not at all."

Brokk looked up and nodded his eyes towards Loki. Brokk's companion, Eitri, was a master craftsman, however Brokk was the smarter and focused of both. "Well then, we'll happily compete against Ivaldi's sons in an athletic contest to the Gods. Also, I am confident that Eitri is going to create higher-quality and better-qualified items than Ivaldi's. However, Loki, let's make this a personal. Isn't it?"

"Can you explain to me what you're planningto do?" Loki inquired.

Brokk declared, "Your head." "If we are victorious in this contest, Loki, we'll get your head. A lot of things are happening inside that head of yours and I'm confident Eitri will develop a wonderful solution from it. Maybe a thinking machine. Another option is it could be an inkwell."

Loki smiled from the outside but was looking grumpy inside. The day had begun with a bang. All he needed to do was ensure Eitri was and Brokk were eliminated from the competition. the gods would receive six amazing presents from dwarfs and Sif would get her beautiful golden hair. He is the best he's capable of. Loki was his name.

He responded, "Of course." "It's in my head. There's nothing to worry about."

The sons of Ivaldi were making their precious stones on the mountain. Loki was not concerned with their protection. However, he needed to ensure the safety of Brokk and Eitri did not, and could not be defeated.

Brokk and Eitri entered the forge. The only light source was the glowing orange glow of charcoal. Eitri pulled a pigskin off the shelves and threw it into the fire. The man explained that "I've kept this the pigskin in case I need it for anything similar to this."

Brokk simply did a simple smile.

"Right," Eitri said. "Brokk, you're operating the bellows. Keep pumping them. It must be hot and I want the temperature to stay hot most the time. If it isn't it won't function. Then, pump it up. "Squeeze."

Brokk began pumping the bellows and squeezing the oxygen-rich air into the core of the forge and then heating it. Brokk had done this several times before. Eitri did not wait until he was sure that everything was to his liking.

In the outside of the forge Eitri worked at his work. A massive black insect came in when Eitri opened the door to go out. It wasn't a deerfly or a horsefly. deerfly. It was larger than both. It flew in and then swung around all over the area in a terrifying way.

In the outside of the forge Brokk heard Eitri's Hammers, and the sound of filing, shaping, twisting and banging.

Brokk's hands were stung by an enormous black fly. It was the largest fly you've ever witnessed.

Brokk was holding two hands on the bellows. He didn't get his hands off the pump in order to strike the fly. Brokk was bit on the back of his hand by an insect.

Brokk continued to shake his fists.

Eitri came through the wide door, and carefully removed the pieces of the work off the forge. It was an enormous boar, with sparkling bristles made of gold.

"Wonderful job," Eitri said. "If the temperature was only a fraction more or less cold, then the whole event was unproductive."

"You were very good also," Brokk said.

This black fly which was perched in the ceiling's corner was furious and angry.

Eitri put the gold block upon the iron forge. He declared, "Correct." "This one will smash them all. Begin to pump the bellows as I make a call. Whatever happens do not stop, speed down or stop. There's plenty of fiddly work to be accomplished."

Brokk told me, "I got it."

Eitri left the room and headed to work. Brokk was silent until Eitri's voice came through before he began to pump the bellows.

The black fly was swooping onto Brokk's neck after having circling the room carefully. The atmosphere was hot, and tightly sealed inside the furnace, the bug was able to move away gently to escape an icy puddle of sweat. Brokk's neck was bit in the strongest way it could. Brokk's work was stained by blood scarlet, however, the dwarf was still pumping.

Eitri reappeared. He returned from the forge and picked up an arm-ring with a white hot. To cool it down then he put it in the stone cooling tub of the forge. The arm-ring broke into the form of a steam cloud as it fell into the ocean. The ring was quickly cool changing from red to orange hot, then gold as it cools.

"It's called Draupnir," Eitri said.

"Do You mean that dripper?" Brokk said, "That's a funny name for the loop."

"Not to be used for the one you have," Eitri said, when he showed Brokk what was so unique about the arm-ring.

"Now," Eitri said, "there's something I've wanted to create for quite a while." This is my greatest work. However, it is more complicated than the two other ones. Here's what you need to accomplish"

Brokk told him, "Pump and don't stop pumping?"

"You're right," Eitri said. "More than ever before. Do not let your speed drop because otherwise, the whole thing could be destroyed." Eitri carried an iron ingot from a pig into the forge. It was more massive than any other iron ingot that the Black Fly (who is Loki) has ever seen before.

He left his room, and verbally signaled Brokk to pump.

Brokk was beginning to pump and Eitri's hammers began to audible as Eitri pulled shaped the, welded and joined.

Loki in the form of a fly has decided that being subtle was not an option anymore. Eitri's art work was enough to impress gods. And if gods were sufficiently pleased Loki would be able to lose his head. Loki was swooping down on Brokk's eyes, and started biting the eyes of the dwarf. The dwarf was able to get his heart pumping despite the pain inside his eyes. Loki was able to sink his teeth into every time, more intensely speedier, more forcefully. Blood was now flowing from the eyelids of the dwarf, through his eyes, and then down his face completely blinding him.

Brokk was looking at his chin and shaking his head in an effort to shake off the fly. The head was jerked between his sides. He turned his mouth around and tried to blast his head at the fly. It ended up being a disaster. The fly bit again at the dwarf only the dwarf was able to see blood. His head was filled with intense pain.

Brokk took a moment to count, then lifted one of his hands from the bellows before swiping at the same time with such speed and force that Loki barely made it out from the danger of his own life. Brokk took the bellows back and started to pump.

Eitri declared, "Enough!"

The black fly flew across the bed in a shaky manner. It was then able fly away when Eitri was able to open the door.

Eitri was depressed when he saw his brother. Brokk's face was covered in sweat and blood. "I'm not sure of what you were up to that day," Eitri said. "However you came very close to ruining everything. At the end of the day, the temperatures were all over the range. It isn't as spectacular as I would have hoped. We'll just have time and check back to."

Loki was seen entering through the open door dressed in Loki form. "Are you prepared to compete?" he asked.

"Brokk will travel to Asgard and present my offerings to the gods, while shaving off your hair," Eitri said. "I am a fan of making things most at the forge I have built."

Brokk appeared to look Loki in the eye with swelling eyes. Brokk declared, "I'm looking forward to cutting off your a$$." "It was a personal issue."

II

Three gods were seated on their seats in Asgard One-eyed Odin All-father red-bearded Thor Thunder King, and gorgeous Frey the god of summer's harvest. The gods would be those who make the final decision.

Loki stood in front of them along with Ivaldi's three almost identical sons. Brook stood on his own in the corner with his dark beard and brooding appearance with his possessions hidden behind covers.

"So," Odin explained. "How can we tell what's looking at?"

Loki declared, "Treasures." "The children of Ivaldi have presented items to your including the great Odin and the gods of Thor, Frey, Eitri and Brokk. It is your responsibility to decide which of the six items you consider the most useful. I personally will show you the items created by the sons of Ivaldi's."

The king presented Odin his Gungnir spear. It was a gorgeous spear, with elaborate rune engravings.

"It can get through anything and be able to find its target when the ball is thrown," Loki said. In the end, Odin did not have a second eye and his aim may be a bit unstable at times. "An swearing ceremony made upon that spear, however other hand, is not breakable."

Odin held the spear. He declared, "It's perfect."

"And this is a raging hair of golden hair" Loki boasted. It's made of real gold. It can be connected to the hair of the person who is in need, grow it, and behave as if it were hair that is natural in all ways. "A 100 thousand gold hair strands."

"I'll test it," Thor said. testing," Thor declared. "Come here, Sif."

Sif stood up and went toward the front, keeping her head tucked away. The head scarf was taken off. When the gods saw her hairless, pink, and hair, she delicately put the gold dwarfs' hair on her head. She shaking her hair, which caused gods to exhale. They sat in awe as the wig's lace-ups connected to her scalp and the next moment, Sif came out before them, more beautiful and gorgeous than before.

"Impressive," Thor exclaimed. "Way you go!"

Sif put her golden locks into the air, and then stepped out in the sun to show off her new style.

The final of Ivaldi's remarkable gifts to his sons was small and folded as linen. Loki put this cloth before Frey.

"Can you describe the name of this item?" Unimpressed Frey stated, "It is like a silky scarf."

Loki said, "It does." "However when you take it apart and you'll be able to see it's a submarine dubbed Skidbladnir. Anywhere it goes, there'll always be a pleasant breeze. It is the biggest ship that you could ever imagine, it folds into a cloth such as it is. that it can be stuffed in your pocket."

Loki was happy Loki was happy, and Frey was amazed. It was a beautiful trio of presents. Brokk was the next to receive them. Brokk had a huge insect bite on the inside of his mouth. Also, his eyelids were swollen and red. Brokk appeared at Loki to be way too confident, especially when you consider the accomplishments of Ivaldi's sons.

Brokk grabbed the golden arm-ring and set it before Odin at the throne of his highest rank. "This arm-ring is known as Draupnir," said Brokk. "Because every night at 9 o'clock eight gold arm-rings with identical beauty will pour out of it. You can offer rewards to people by giving the ring or store them as well, and the value of your possessions will grow."

Odin was looking at the arm-ring, then placed it on his arm. It was over his biceps. The ring sparkled there. "It is amazing," he said.

Loki was able to recall the fact that Odin had said the exact thing regarding the spear.

Brokk came across to Frey. He shook a cloth and revealed a massive boar that had bristles made of gold.

"This is the boar that my brother designed for you for pulling your horse" Brokk explained. Brokk. "It will run across the sky, and over the ocean, quicker than the most powerful horse. There is never a night so dark that it's golden bristles won't give the illusion of light and let you know what you're doing. It is never tired and will never let you down. It's known as Gullenbursti The golden-bristled one."

Frey seemed amazed. However, Loki, the magical ship that folded into cloth, was as amazing as the unbestoppable boar shining in the darkness. Loki's head was fairly secured. The last present Brokk needed to give was one that Loki knew he'd already been able to destroy.

Under the cloth, Brokk created a hammer and put it before Thor.

Thor took a look and looked around and sniffed.

"The handle is quite small," he said.

Brokk smiled. "Yes," he said. "That's me to blame. I was working on the bellows. However, before you throw it out I'll tell you what makes this hammer special. It's known as Mjollnir The lightning-maker. In the first place, it's impervious to breakage. It doesn't matter how much you strike objects with it the hammer will remain intact."

Thor seemed to be curious. Thor had broken many weapons throughout the years mostly by striking objects with them.

"If you throw the hammer at it, it will never miss whatever you aim it at."

Thor was even more curious. He had lost a number of great weapons after throwing them at things that annoyed him, and then vanishing. He was able to watch too numerous weapons he threw disappear in the distance, not to be returned to.

"No regardless of how long or hard your throw, the ball will be returned to your hands."

Thor was smiling now. The thunder god did not usually smile. "You can alter your size for the Hammer. It will expand, and it will also get smaller to a size that, if you would like, you could put it in you shirt."

Thor was able to clap his hands in joy and thunder echoed throughout Asgard.

"And yet as you've observed," concluded Brokk sadly, "the handle of the Hammer is actually too long. My error. I didn't keep the bellows on when my younger brother Eitri made it."

"The hand's shortness is a minor cosmetic issue," said Thor. "This Hammer will shield us from the giants of frost. This is the best present I've ever received."

"It will defend Asgard. It will also protect everyone else," said Odin with his approval.

"If I was a gigantic I'd be scared of Thor should he have the hammer," Frey said. Frey.

"Yes. It's a fantastic Hammer. But Thor is what? What about the hair? Sif's beautiful , new, gold hair!" said Loki very desperately.

"What? Oh, yes. My wife has beautiful hair." stated Thor. "Now. I'll show you how to increase the size of the hammer as well as shrink. Brokk."

"Thor's Hammer is more powerful than my amazing spear and my amazing arm-ring,"" said Odin and nodded.

"The Hammer is bigger and more powerful than my ship or my boar,"" said Frey. "It keeps the gods of Asgard in peace."

The gods were able to clap Brokk to the side and informed Brokk that Eitri as well as Eitri had created the most obedient gift they've ever received.

"Good to be aware of," said Brokk. He looked at Loki. "So," said Brokk. "I am going to take your head off the son of Laufey and take it back to me. Eitri is going to be thrilled. We can make it into something beneficial."

"I . . . will ransom my head," said Loki. "I have treasures to offer you." "Eitri and I have everything we require," said Brokk. "We create treasures. No, Loki. I'd like your head."

Loki was thinking for a while before saying, "Then you can have it. If you can get me to stop." And Loki ran up into the air and flew off, way over their heads. Within moments, he was gone.

Brokk turned to Thor. "Can you catch him?"

Thor smiled and sighed. "I should not," he said. "But I would really like to try with the Hammer."

Within a few seconds, Thor returned and was in a moment, holding Loki with his hands. Loki was looking at him with inexplicably furious anger.

The dwarf Brokk was armed with a knife. "Come Here, Loki," he told him. "I'm going to take your head off."

"Of of course,"" Loki said. Loki. "You could cut my head off. However, and I'm appealing to the the mighty Odin in this instance--if you cut off one part of me's necks then you are in violation of our agreement. We promises you my head and my head alone."

Odin tilted his head. "Loki does not lie," Odin said. "You are not entitled to cut off his neck."

Brokk was upset. "But I can't take off the top of his head, without cutting it in half." Brokk said.

Loki seemed content with himself. "You can see," he said, "if people pondered the preciseness of their statements they wouldn't think of taking on Loki the smartest and most intelligent and the most difficult, the most intelligent, the prettiest . . ." Brokk whispered an idea to Odin. "That is reasonable," agreed Odin. Brokk made a strip of leather and knife. He put the leather in a ring

Loki's mouth. Brokk attempted to cut the leather with the point of the knife's blade. "It's no good," said Brokk. "My knife isn't cutting you."

"I may have thought of arranging to shield myself from knives," said Loki modestly. "Just in case the whole you-can't-cut-my-neck ploy did not work. I'm afraid that there is no knife blade that can slice me!"

Brokk grunted and released an awl. It was an awl that was a pointed spike, which is employed in leatherwork. He he smashed it into the leather, making holes in Loki's lips. Then , he grabbed a thick thread and stitched Loki's lips to the thread.

Brokk left after which he left Loki in a state of discontent, his lips shut and unable to voice his displeasure.

For Loki his pain of not being able to speak is more painful than the discomfort being able to have his mouth sewn in the leather.

You now know that This can be the reason why gods acquired their most amazing treasures. It was the fault of Loki. The hammer of Thor was also Loki's responsibility. That's the thing with Loki. You hated him regardless of when most grateful. You were grateful to Loki even when you disliked Loki the most.

Chapter 3: The Master Builder

Thor was on his way towards the east to fight Trolls. Without Thor, Asgard was quieter, however, it was not protected. The first time Asgard was attacked shortly after the Aesir-Vanir agreement, when gods were still in the process of establishing their own kingdoms, Asgard was not protected.

"We cannot always rely upon Thor," Odin said. "We require protection. Giants are headed our way. Trolls are heading their way."

Heimdall Goddall, the god's watchman, said "What would you like to propose?"

"A wall,"" Odin explained. "It's sufficient to keep giants of frost away. It's thick enough to ensure that even the most powerful troll would not be able to pass through it."

"Building such a tall and deep wall will take us many months," Loki said.

Odin acknowledged the fact smiling. "But," he said, "we do need a wall."

A newcomer came into Asgard the following day. He was a tall man in a blacksmith's costume and he was accompanied by an enormous gray stallion that had long back.

The person who was talking to the stranger said "They claim that you require to put up a wall."

"Go forward," Odin said.

The man said, "I can create you an obstacle." "Make it tall enough that even the biggest giant could not reach it, and thick enough that even the most powerful troll wouldn't be able to penetrate it. I'll build it so efficiently that I can layer stone upon stone, that even an Ant will be able walk through it. I'll construct a wall for you that will last for a millennium."

"Building such a wall is likely to require a lot of time," Loki said.

"Not in any way," the stranger replied. "I'll be able to complete this in the three seasons. It's the first winter day. will be next week. It will only take me one winter, one summer and a winter to build."

"And What would you like to ask for a bargain if you were able to accomplish the same?" Odin wondered. "

"I only require three things to exchange what I'm offering," the man explained. In the first place, I'd like to get married the beautiful lady Freya." "That will be not a small thing," Odin said. "It would not be a surprise to think that Freya might have thoughts on the matter as well. What are the other two things? "

The man flashed a confident smile. "If I construct your wall, I'd like Freya's back, along with the sun that shines through the sky at daytime and the moon that provides us nighttime illumination," he said. If I construct your wall, gods will give me these three items."

Freya attracted the attention of the gods. She didn't speak but the lips of her mouth were pursed while her eyes red with fury. The hair was swathed in gold, and it was as bright as her hair and she was wearing the Brisings necklace on her neck. It shone like northern lights when it touched her face.

"Go out and sit," Odin advised the stranger. The man then left but not before asking where he could find water and food for his horse, Svadilfari, which means "one who is prone to unfortunate circumstances."

Odin rub his temples using his fingers. He then turned his back to all the gods.

"How do you manage?" Odin was perplexed.

The gods began talking to each other.

Odin shouted, "Quiet!" "One at one at a time!" says the narrator.

Every god and goddesses held their own opinion on the matter, and they all agreed: Freya, the sun and moon were far too essential and valuable to be given to someone else even though he was able to build the wall they needed in the three seasons.

Freya has a different perspective. She believed that the man should be punished for his obstinacy, and then exiled from Asgard and taken away.

"So," Odin the All-Father told me, "we've made our decision." "No," we respond.

55

A dry cough was heard out of the hallway's corner. The gods looked around to see who was coughing and it was a cough intended to draw attention. They were able to see Loki and he responded to their gazes with smile and raised his finger as if there was something to have to say.

"It is important to point out that you're not noticing something important," he said.

"I do not think we've missed anything, troublemaker of gods," Freya said sarcastically.

"You're all overlooking the fact," he said, "that the idea this person proposes is simply impossible." There is no way anyone alive today could build an imposing wall as high and as thick as that he described in just 18 months. It's something only deities or a giant could accomplish, not to mention mortal men. I'd bet my life on it."

The gods all sighed, grunted and looked awestruck when they heard this. with the exception of Freya who looked angry. "You're an entire bunch of knuckleheads,"" Freya said. "Especially Loki, Loki, who thinks you're genius."

"What the man claims that he is able to accomplish isn't an easy undertaking," Loki said. This is what I'm proposing that we accept the price and demands of his client however we place strict requirements on him that he doesn't have any financial support to build his walland only has one year to complete the work in lieu of the three. We will not pay him in the event that any part of the wall is not completed at the beginning of summer, and that is expected to be."

Heimdall was asked, "Why would he consent to this?"

Frey who is Freya's brother asked, "And what benefit does the wall provide us in comparison to not having any walls at all?"

Loki tried to control his anger. Are all gods in a knucklehead's way? The man began explaining his thoughts as like he was speaking to a child. "The smith is going to begin creating his wall. The smith won't finish the work. In the course of a fool's errand you can work for free over the course of six months. After six months we'll eject him--we may even beat him up for his arrogance. We'll then use everything that he's achieved up to now as the base to build the wall in the next few years. We're not in danger of losing Freya and the moon or the sun."

"Why did he consent to building it during an entire time of year?" Tyr the God of War, pondered.

Loki suggested "He could not confirm it."

"However He appears confident and confident and is not hesitant to accept an opportunity."

All the gods shook their heads and smacked Loki in the back and told Loki that he was a skilled and clever man as well as that it was great that the man was clever and in their favor because now they'd have their foundations set at no cost. They each congratulated one another on their intelligence and negotiation skills.

Freya did not speak. She was fidgeting with her delicate necklace, with Brisings present. It was the seal, this was the exact necklace Loki took from her while she was bathing. Heimdall struggled with Loki with a seal to get it back to her. She had doubts about Loki. She wasn't pleased by the way the conversation taken place.

The gods summoned the creator into their the throne room.

He turned his back to Gods. They appeared to be happy with laughter and kissing one another. Freya On the contrary, didn't smile.

"How do I know? " the builder asked.

Loki told Loki, "You asked for three seasons." "We're going to give you only one season. First day of winter will be today. If you fail to finish the wall on that first summer day, you'll be fired. If you build the wall as tall as it is thick, strong, and impregnable as we have decided to build it, you will receive everything you requested which includes the moon, sun, and Freya. There will be no help in building your wall. You must construct this wall by yourself."

for a short period of time the stranger was silent. He seemed to be considering Loki's demands and words while he gazed off towards the distance. He then shook his head and looked towards the Gods. "You declared that I would not receive any assistance from outside. I'd like Svadilfari my horse to aid me in bringing the stones herethat I'll use to construct the wall. It doesn't seem to be an unjust request."

"It isn't unreasonable," Odin agreed, and the gods of other gods nodded and acknowledged that horses were capable of carrying heavy stones.

They made oaths which were the most powerful of vows in which neither side could sacrifice the other, the gods or the stranger. They claimed that their arms that Draupnir Odin's arm-ring made of gold and Gungnir

Odin's sword as well as an oath that was sworn to Gungnir were indestructible.

The gods watched the man's work on the following day when the sun began to rise. He spit on his hands before he began digging the trench in which the first stone would be erected.

Heimdall said, "He mines deep."

Frey the brother of Freya told her, "He digs hard."

"Well obviously, the man is an incredibly trench-digger and ditch-digger," said the narrator.

Loki is reluctantly in agreement. "However think about the amount of stones he'll need to carry to the hills. The process of digging a trench only one thing. It's quite another thing to carry stones for hundreds of miles without assistance and then stack them one stone over one another and so tightly packed that there is no way for even an ant to get between them to construct a wall that is taller than the largest gigantic."

Freya was able to give Loki an angry look, but didn't say anything.

As the sun set was over, the builder climbed on his horse and headed towards the mountains in search of his first stones. The horse carried an empty stoneboat in its wake. A sled of a low size dragged through the bone-soft Earth. The gods watched them depart. The moon was bright and pale in the early winter sky.

"He will return within a week," Loki added. Loki. "I am interested to see the amount of rocks this horse is able to carry. It seems sturdy."

The gods were in their hall of feasts and there was a lot of joy and laughter, however Freya didn't laugh.

It began to snow at dawn, a slight dusting of snowflakes. It was a glimpse of the snows deep which would continue into the winter.

Heimdall who could see all that was coming towards Asgard and did not miss a single thing and woke the gods from the darkness.

They gathered around the trench that a stranger had dug earlier in the day. As the dawn gathered they saw the builder riding alongside his horse as he walked towards them.

The horse was constantly moving a number of granite blocks that were enough that the sled left deep ruts through deep black Earth.

The man recognized gods, he made a gesture and wished them a good morning. He pointed towards the rising sun and then he smirked at gods. He then loosened him from his rock and let it run free before he began to twirl the first stones of granite into the trench he already dug in order to take it in.

"The horse is certainly robust," said Balder, most beautiful of the Aesir. "No normal horse would be able to carry rocks this heavy."

"It is much stronger than we thought," said Kvasir the wise.

"Ah," said Loki. "The horse is going to tire soon. It was its first day at work. It isn't going

63

to be able haul so many stones at night. Then winter is about to arrive. It will snow thick and heavy and the blizzards could be overwhelming and getting to the mountain will be a challenge. There's nothing to be worried about. Everything is happening according to plan."

"I love you to pieces," said Freya, who was unable to smile with Loki. She left for Asgard at dawn but did not stop to watch the stranger construct the foundations for his wall.

Each night the construction worker, the horse, along with the empty stone-boat departed for the mountains. Every morning, they returned with the horse pulling another twenty granite blocks, each block being bigger than the man with the highest height.

Each day , the wall grew in size, and by the evening, it had grown larger and more intimidating than when it first appeared.

Odin made a request to the gods for Odin to.

"The walls are growing rapidly," he said. "And we took an irreparable swearing oath, a ring-oath and a weapon-oath that when he is finished building his wall by the time he is due we'll grant him the sun and moon, and also the hand in marriage to Freya the gorgeous." Kvasir The wise one stated, "No man can do the things that this master builder is doing. I think he might be more than a human being." "A massive," said Odin. "Perhaps."

"If only Thor was there," sighed Balder.

"Thor is hammering trolls far away in the east,"" Odin said. Odin. "And even should he return the oaths we swear to are strong as well as binding."

Loki tried to comfort the people. "We are just like old ladies who are constantly worried about nothing. The builder will not be able to finish his wall prior to the beginning of summer, even though you are the most powerful big king on earth. It's not possible." "I I wish Thor was there," said Heimdall. "He would be able to figure out the best way to go."

The snows fell, however, the deep snow didn't hinder the wall-builder and it didn't slow Svadilfari his horse. The gray stallion dragged his sled, which was laden with stones, through snowdrifts and blizzards, over steep hills, and then down through the icy ravines.

The days started to become longer.

The sun rose earlier every morning. The snows started to melt and the the mud was heavy and heavy, like the kind that sticks onto your shoes and pulls your feet down.

"The horse is not able to drag those rocks into the water," said Loki. "They will sink and the horse will fall off his feet."

However, Svadilfari was steadfast and unflinching even in the most thick wet mud. He towed the rocks to Asgard in spite of the fact that the stone-boat was so massive it caused deep gashes to the hills' sides. The builder was now transporting the stones hundreds of feet while he pushed each one into its proper the right spot.

The mud was dried and the spring blooms came out: coltsfoot, yellow, and wood anemones of white blooming in a flurry. the wall that was being constructed around Asgard was an enthralling and impressive thing. Once it was completed the wall would be impervious and no large, no troll or no dwarf, and no mortal could ever break through the wall. The man who built it continued to construct it with unending good humor. He did not appear to mind if it rained or snowed or not, neither was his horse. They would haul the stones from the mountains. Every day, they laid the granite blocks on the layer before.

It was now the final day of winter as the walls were nearly finished.

The gods sat upon their the thrones in Asgard They also spoke.

"The sun,"" declared Balder. "We are giving away sun."

"We put an astronomical moon on the top of the sky in order to mark off the days and months of the year," said Bragi poet god with a moody. "Now there is there will be no moon."

"And Freya, what would we do without Freya?" asked Tyr.

"If the builder you're talking about is massive," said Freya, with the sound of ice "then I'll marry him and take him back to Jotunheim It is interesting to determine the one I'm more angry at, the builder for taking me away, or everyone else for donating the me over to him."

"Now Don't do this," began Loki, however Freya interrupted Loki, and she said, "If this giant does capture me, as well as the moon and the sun and all the stars, then I'm asking just one request from gods in Asgard."

"Name this," said Odin all-father who had never spoken up to now.

"I would want to see those who were responsible for this tragedy to die prior to my departure," said Freya. "I believe it is fair. If I'm going to go into the realm of the giants in frost in which the sun and moon will be sucked out of the sky, and the entire world sink into darkness forever The existence of the person who brought us here must be thrown away."

"Ah," said Loki. "The assigning blame is a challenge. Who can remember exactly who suggested the idea? In my memory that all gods are equally in this mistake. We all recommended it. We all agreed."

"You recommended it,"" told Freya. "You got these people to agree to the idea. And I'll be seeing your dead by the time I quit Asgard."

"We all" started Loki and he sat down to see the the faces of gods in the hall and then he sat down in silence.

"Loki the son of Laufey," said Odin, "this is the result of your poor advice." "And the result was as bad as your other tips," said Balder. Loki gave him a bitter glance.

"We must have the builder lose his bet," said Odin. "Without breaching the vow. He has to be in breach."

"I do not know what I should expect you to do ," told Loki.

"I don't want to receive anything in return," Odin said. Odin. "But If this builder succeeds in completing his wall at the end of tomorrow, your demise will be long and painful and an unhonorable death for that."

Loki was looking at the gods from one to the next and, in each of their faces Loki saw his own death as well as anger and regret. He didn't see forgiveness or mercy.

It's a gruesome death, indeed. What would be the alternative? What was he able to do? He was not able to strike at the builder. But on the other hand . . .

Loki smiled. "Leave this for me."

He walked out of the hall and no one gods attempted to stop him from walking.

The builder was finished putting his stones onto the walls. Tomorrow in the summer's first day, just as the sun set, the wall would be completed before he could go home to Asgard with his earnings. Just twenty granite blocks left. He climbed the wooden scaffolding, which was rough and called out to his horse.

Svadilfari was walking in the same way he always did in the thick grass close to the forest, about half a mile away from the walls, however he only was there when his master whistled.

The builder snatched the ropes he had tied to the stone boat and began to tie it to his gray horse. The sun was still low on the horizon, however it wouldn't be set for a long time and the disc of the moon was dull however, it was there high in the sky, too. Soon, both will be in his possession, the better light , and the less beautiful and Freya the woman who was prettier than the sun or the moon. The builder could not take his prize before they were his. He had been working so hard and for so long throughout winter . . .

He whistled for his horse again. It was odd that he never had to repeat his whistle twice. He could be able to see Svadilfari as he shook his head and running around in the wildflowers in the meadow in spring. The horse would make a small step forward and then take a step back as if it could smell something appealing in the warm breeze of the evening, but he was unable to determine the smell. "Svadilfari!" called the builder. The horse's ears were pricked and began a quick sprint across the meadow in the direction of the builder.

The builder sat back and watched his horse face him and he was satisfied. The horses' hoofbeats were booming over the grass, increasing and then doubling again with the echo which bounced off the gray granite wall. So for a brief second, the builder thought that a large group of horses were coming towards him.

The builder thought that it was just one horse.

He looked at his head and was aware of his error. He didn't have a horse. There was not a single hoofbeat. Two . . .

Another horse, however, was chestnut-colored. The builder recognized that the mare was right away. He didn't have to check behind her to see her legs. Every single line or even a single inch every aspect of the chestnut was female. Svadilfari was able to turn as he ran through the meadow, and then slowing down, he reared up, and yelled out loudly.

The chestnut mare was uninterested in the man. She stopped her running like he wasn't there. She sat down and appeared to be mowing in the grass when Svadilfari was approaching her. However, once he got just a few yards away her, she started to sprint away from him. It was a slow canter which soon turned into a gallop as the graystallion raced behind her trying to keep her in line at least a length or two behind, and nipping at her tail and rump with his teeth but never getting there.

They raced through the meadow in the golden, creamy light of day, the gray horse and brown, sweaty, gleaming on their backs. It was almost like dancing.

The builder clapped his hands in a loud way while he whistled and yelled Svadilfari's number, however, the stallion resisted.

The builder fled with the intention of catching the horse and return him to his senses, however the chestnut mare appeared to be aware of what he was trying to accomplish as she slowed down and put her ears and her mane against the back of the stallion's head. She then ran, as if the wolves were following her towards an edge in the woods. Svadilfari chased her and within a few seconds, they both disappeared into the shadows of the forest.

The builder cursed, spat, then waited for his horse's return.

The shadows grew longer the shadows grew longer, and Svadlifari was not able to return.

He returned home to the boat. He gazed into the woods. Then , he washed his hands and then took hold of the ropes and began to drag the boat made of stone across the grassy meadow and flowers of spring towards the quarry in the mountains.

He didn't return until the time of dawn. It was sun-rise up over the sky by the time the builder made his way back to Asgard and threw the stone boat in his back.

There were ten stone blocks on the stone-boat, as much as the way he could and was hauling and heaving the stone-boat , and cursing at the stones, but with every move, he was further away from the wall.

Beautiful Freya was standing at the gate looking at him.

"You have just 10 stone blocks," she told him. "You will require twice as number of bricks to build the wall."

The builder didn't say anything. He continued to carry his blocks towards the gateway that was not finished with his face hidden behind covered in a mask. There was no smile or winks, not anymore.

"Thor returns from east,"" Freya told him. "He will be here with us in the near future." As the gods of Asgard stood by to observe the builder when he carried the stones towards the wall. They stood with Freya and surrounded her, and surrounded her.

They were silent at first before they started to laugh and smile and ask questions.

"Hey!" shouted Balder. "You only get to see the sun if you complete the wall. Do you think that you'll take the sun to take it with you?"

"And Moon," said Bragi. "Such it's a shame that you did not have your horse on your side. He could have transported all the rocks you'll need."

The gods laughed.

The builder released the boat of stone. He walked up to the gods. "You have cheated!" he said, and his face was red in anger and arousal.

"We haven't cheated," said Odin. "No more than you've committed a fraud. Do you think we would allowed you to build our wall had we suspected that you were a monster?"

The builder grabbed the rock with one hand and then crushed it against another cutting the granite block into two. He looked to the godswith half the stone held in each hand. Now the builder was thirty, twenty or fifty foot tall. His face turned twisted. did not look like the person who was in Asgard the previous year peaceful and calm. His face was now the face of a granite rock, bent and sculpted with anger and hatred.

"I am an enormous mountain," he said. "And your gods are nothing more than cheats and oath-breakers who are vile. If I was riding my horse I'd have finished your wall by today. I would take the beautiful Freya and the sun as well as the moon to earn my living. I'd be leaving you in the darkness and the frigid cold, without even beauty to cheer you up."

"No swearing was violated," said Odin. "But no oath will save you from our wrath now."

It roared in fury and fled towards the gods, carrying a huge piece of granite was placed on each hand to form the shape of a club.

The gods were silent until the giant could see that was standing in front of them. A massive god, with a red-bearded face and a muscular physique sporting iron gauntlets with an iron hammer that he was swinging at times. He released the hammer as it was pointed at the huge.

Lightning flashes shot from the clear sky then followed by a low, thumping sound of thunder when Thor's hammer fell from his hand.

The giant of the mountain saw the hammer growing in size as it sped towards him. Then he could not have seen anything else ever again.

The gods had completed building the wall by themselves, but it took many weeks to cut and move the remaining ten blocks out of the high-quality quarries in the mountains, then bring the blocks back down to Asgard and put them on the highest point of the gate. They weren't as well-designed or sized as the blocks that the master builder had designed and set up his own.

The gods thought that they should have allowed the giant to grow closer to completing his wall, before Thor took him down. Thor declared that he was glad to see gods having entertainment waiting for him once Thor returned home in the west.

It was odd, because it was very different from Loki, Loki was not around to be celebrated for his role in pulling off Svadilfari. Svadilfari. While some reported the magnificent chestnut mare that was seen in the meadows under Asgard however, no one was able to pinpoint exactly where he was. Loki went missing for the majority of the year, and when he came back and was joined by an unnamed gray foal.

It was a stunning foal, even though it had 8 legs, instead of four. It also was with Loki everywhere he traveled. It kissed him and took care of Loki like he was its mother. This, naturally was the situation.

The foal was born into a horse named Sleipnir, a massive gray stallion that was the fastest and most muscular horse ever been, or could ever be and a horse capable of outrunning the winds.

Loki gave Sleipnir the god of horses to Odin as a gift. the greatest horse of gods and men.

A lot of people admire Odin's horse. However, only the bravest of people would mention its parents at Loki's beckoning but nobody would dare to make a second mention of it. Loki would make a point to make you feel uncomfortable should you be heard talking about how he got Svadlifari away from his master, and then saved gods from his horrible concept. Loki took his anger to heart.

This is the tale about how gods gained their wall.

Chapter 4: The Children Of Loki

Loki was conscious of his beauty. People were eager to believe in him but he was a fraud and self-centered at the best, and reckless or malicious at the worst. He was married to Sigyn. She was gorgeous and happy who was a beautiful and happy woman, after Loki got married and courted her, but appeared to still be waiting for negative news. He gave him an child, Narfi, and another son, Vali, not long after.

Loki often disappeared for long periods , and then never come back, and Sigyn appears to be waiting for the worst news, yet Loki appeared unsteady and guilty, and still appear as if quite happy with himself.

He left three times and every time he returned.

Odin summoned Loki for the third time when Odin returned to Asgard.

A wise, old-fashioned one-eyed God declared, "I have dreamed a dream." "You have an entire family."

"My Name is Narfi as I'm the dad of an infant. Vali is a good boy, who is respectful and sane, even though I have to admit that he may not always obey the father."

"Not the kids!" declares the voice. Loki you're the mother of three more children. You've been sneaking off to spend your nights and days with Angrboda the giantess from the world of giants made of ice. Also, she is the mother of three children. I've observed them in my head when I sleep and my dreams have warned me that they'll be God's greatest enemies in the near future."

Loki was silent. He tried to look embarrassed, but the best did he could do was appear content with himself.

Odin invoked gods which were led by Tyr and Thor and announced to them that they'd be travelling through Jotunheim and Giantland to bring Loki's children back to Asgard.

The gods traveled to the realm of the giants, overcame many obstacles along the way to Angrboda's house. She didn't expect them and had let her children play in her hall to play together. When the gods saw how happy Loki and Angrboda's kids were shocked however, it did not hinder them from. They grabbed them and tied them up, carrying the oldest child and tied to the naked branch from a pine tree and then snuffing the second one with an encased willow muzzle. They tied a rope to its neck to form it was a collar and the child followed with a dark and unsettling.

On the right side from the 3rd child could see a beautiful young woman, whereas those who were left did not want to look at her since they could see a decomposing woman walking around them with her flesh and skin turned into black.

"Did you hear something?" On the third day of their return into the land of giants of frost, Thor inquired of Tyr. Tyr rubs Loki's second child's soft neck with his huge right hand while they slept over the course of the night inside a tiny clearing.

"Wait, what?"

"The giants aren't believed to have been watching us. Their mother hasn't even scoured us. They seem to want to keep Loki's children out of Jotunheim."

Tyr was adamant, "That is foolish talk," but he shivered while he spoke it in spite of the warm flames.

After two day of tiring and exhausting journeys they reached Odin's hall.

Tyr immediately said, "These are Loki's children."

Loki's first child was tied by a tree. It it grew to be larger that the tree it tied. Jormungundr was its name and it was a serpent. Tyr said, "It has grown several feet since the time we've carried this back."

"Be careful," Thor cautioned. It could release a fiery black poison. It spewed venom on me however it didn't hurt me. This is why its head was tied by the branch in this way."

"It is a baby," Odin explained. "It's expanding. We'll move it to a place that will not harm anyone."

Odin released Jormungundr from the shore of the sea above all water The sea that runs around Midgard and watched it slip and sway beneath the waves, while swimming with curls and loops.

Odin was watching the object until it disappeared over the horizon. He was unsure if he taken the right choice. He had no idea. He followed the instructions of his dreams However, not even the most wise of gods has more knowledge than they do.

The snake rose until it was encircling the earth in the ocean's gray waters. ocean. Jormungundr is also known for its role as the Midgard snake.

After Odin came back to his grand hall when he returned, he instructed Loki's daughter that she should move in the right direction.

The right-hand side of her face her cheeks were white and pink Her eye was green as

Loki's while her lips appeared carmine and full; to her left the skin was striated and blotched and swollen from the bruising of death. her eyes were rotted and pale, her lips were swollen and spread across her skull-brown teeth.

The father-in-law asked, "What do they name you girl?"

"If you like it All-father, they'll will call me Hel," she said. "You are a courteous child," Odin observed. "I'll give the prize for you."

Hel did not speak; the only thing she said was stare at him with a single green eye that was as clear as an ice chip and her pale face dull and spoiled, and dead. He did not see any fear in her.

He asked the child "Are you still alive?" "Are you alive or dead?"

She said, "I am just myself, Hel, daughter of Angrboda and Loki." "Of any dead person, I like them most. They're not difficult to understand and they address me in a respectful way. "The Living are thoroughly disgusted with me."

Odin thought about the girl's appearance and remembered his hopes. "This child will become ruler of the deepest of the dark places and also the dead from all the realms of existence," Odin continued. She will be the king of those unfortunate souls who die through unjust causes like illness, old age, birth injuries or even childbirth. The warriors who die in battle are still able to return into Valhalla to be revived. Her people, on other hand, will be the dead , who will die in various forms, and be with her in her dark."

Hel smiled a bit for the first time since she'd been separated from her mother.

Odin took Hel down into the darkness without light. He led her to the space where she could receive the people she wanted to serve and then watch her collect her belongings. "I'm going to call the bowl I'm using Hunger," Hel declared. She pulled her knife. "This is called"famine. Also, Sickbed refers to the title given to my bedroom."

Then Angrboda was faced with two children of Loki's. One of them is in the ocean and the other deep within the earth. What else what is to be done in the case of the third?

When they came back to the land of giants, they found the third and youngest of Loki's kids, it was the size of a puppy. Tyr played with its head and neck. He also played with it, taking off its willow muzzle before. This was the wolf's cub grey and black with deep amber-colored eyes.

The wolf cub consumed its food raw, however it could speak like a human in gods and men's language, and was proud of it. Fenrir could be the name given to the small creature.

It was also rapidly growing. It was as big as the wolf at one point and a cave bear the next, and an enormous elk the following day.

Except for Tyr All Gods are afraid of the wolf. He would always play and romp with it, and was the only god who fed the wolf's flesh daily. Every morning, this beast would eat more than it had eaten the day before and, every day it got bigger, stronger and more muscular.

Odin was watching the wolf-child grow in fear because the wolf was always there at the very end of his hopes The last thing Odin had ever seen during any ideas was Fenris Wolf's eyes made of topaz with sharp teeth.

The gods met in an assembly and resolved to join Fenrir at the time of that meeting.

In the forges of the gods they made chains of solid construction and shackles that they used to Fenrir.

The gods shouted, "Here!" as in a way of introducing a brand new game. "Fenrir You've gained so much knowledge in such a short period of time. It's time to put that ability against the wall. We have the strongest chains and shackles available in the world. Do you think that you've got what it takes to break them?"

"I believe that I can," Fenris Wolf said. "Bind to me" is the voice of the narration.

The hands of Fenrir were bound by gods who put huge chains around his body. While they did this, the wolf remained in motion. While they chained the massive Wolf The gods smiled at each other.

Thor yelled, "Now!"

The chains snapped as dry twigs while Fenrir wrestled to stretch his legs.

The wolf whooped with joy and triumph to the heavens. He stated, "I broke your chains." "Keep this in your mind."

The gods declared "We will never forget."

Tyr was able to find the wolf's flesh the next day. Fenrir stated, "I broke the fetters." "I was able to break them."

"You did it," Tyr said.

"Do you believe they'll test me on yet another exam?" Every day, I get stronger and better."

"They'll test you." test again. "I'd place my bet to bet on that," Tyr said.

The the wolf was still rising while the deities were at work on a new set of chains at the smithies. Every chain was heavy enough for a normal man to lift. The strongest metal the gods could come up with for chains was iron that came from the earth, paired with iron from the sky. Dromi became the term that was given to the chains.

The gods carried chains over to Fenrir's bedside.

The eyes of the wolf opened.

He said, "Again?"

"If you are able to be free of the chains that hold you," they said to the gods, "then your fame and power will be acknowledged in every corner of this universe." You will get the glory. If these chains aren't able to support you and your power isn't strong enough, then you is greater than that of the gods and giants."

Fenrir smiled and turned to look at the Dromi chains they were more powerful that any other chains encountered and stronger than the strongest bonds. After a brief moment the wolf uttered the words "There there isn't any glory and no risk without it." "I believe that I can liberate my self from these chains. "Tie me up."

He was tied to a chain.

The big wolf pulled and pulled, but the chains held him in his place. The gods looked at each other, they had a hint of triumph in their eyes. However, the huge wolf began to wiggle and twist to kick his legs and squeeze every muscle and sinew within his body. The teeth flashed, his jaws froze as his eyes lit up as his teeth flashed.

While he was writhing, he grunted. He struggled for everything he owned.

The gods took a step back without a thought but it's a wise choice because the chains broke and then snapped so violently that the fragments exploded in the air high and the gods would discover shackles that had been broken stuck in the sides of huge trees or along the top of the mountain many years to take.

"Yes!" exclaimed Fenrir who roared like a wolf and man to celebrate his victory.

The gods who watched the battle didn't look satisfied with the outcome of the fight The wolf noticed. Tyr isn't among them. Fenrir Loki's son was meditating on the topic, as well as other ones.

As time passed, Fenris Wolf grew more visible and hungry.

Odin was contemplating, pondering and thought about it for a while, then contemplated more. The wisdom of Mimir was his, and so was the knowledge he learned by hanging from the world tree as self-sacrifice. Then, he summoned Frey's messenger, gentle elf Skirnir his side and recognized as the Gleipnir chain. Skirnir accompanied his horse over the bridge of rainbows to Svartalfheim and gave the dwarfs direction on creating the chain unique to all others.

The dwarfs shuddered as they were listening to Skirnir describe the commission and they referred to their price. Skirnir accepted the price, just according to what Odin was instructed regardless of the fact that the dwarfs' cost was too high.

The dwarfs found the necessary ingredients for the Gleipnir's formation.

The dwarfs gathered these six items:

To start, you can trace cats' footsteps.

Second, the mustache of a woman.

And lastly we have mountains' roots.

Not to be left out the sinews of a bear.

Then, there's the breath of a fish.

The bird's spittle is the sixth item on the list.

Gleipnir was created by combining the elements listed above. (You say you've never seen something like this before? No, you haven't. The dwarfs utilized these for their own creations.)

Skirnir was presented with an wooden box from the dwarfs as they completed their work. It was the length of a silken thread, soft and smooth to the feel. It appeared to be translucent and was light in weight.

With his box at close by, the Skirnir made his way home to Asgard. He returned late at late at night, when the sun was set. The gods were amazed when he revealed the things he brought from the workshop of the dwarfs.

The gods gathered at the shores of the Black Lake, to greet Fenrir by his name. He walked in at a staggering speed, just as dogs do when they are called. The gods were awed by his strength and size.

The wolf questioned, "What's going on?"

They said "We have created the strongest bond." "Not even you'll be able crack this bond" claims the storyteller.

The wolf inflated his chest. He boasted with confidence, "I can burst any chains."

Odin showed Gleipnir by extending his fist. Under night, the weapon glowed.

"What?" the wolf demanded. "That is nothing."

The gods pulled it off to prove its strength. They told him "We aren't able to break it."

The wolf stared towards the fine silken band they held between them. It sparkled like a snail's path or moonlight reflecting off the waves He walked away, uninterested.

"No," he said insistently. "Bring me chains Real fetters, massive chains massive in size and let me show my power."

Odin stated, "This is Gleipnir." "It is stronger than chains or shackles. Fenrir Do you feel afraid?"

"Afraid? Absolutely not. But what happens if cut an intricate ribbon? Do you think I'll achieve notoriety and recognition? People would gather to inquire, "Do you realize how powerful and strong Fenris Wolf really is?" He's so powerful, the silken ribbon he broke was shattered in the movie 'The Last Jedi!' The breaking of Gleipnir won't make me look any better."

"You're scared," Odin said.

The enormous beast inhaled a sigh from the air. The wolf muttered, his amber eyes shining in the night, "I smell treachery and deceit." "And even though I am of the opinion that your Gleipnir is just a piece of ribbon and not a binding contract, I'm not willing to be legally bound by it."

"Are you? The one who broke the strongest and biggest chains? "You're scared of this group?" Thor inquired.

The wolf roared, "I am afraid of anything." "I believe that you are scared of me because you are small creatures."

Odin was rubbing his bearded cheeks. "You're not a liar, Fenrir. There's nothing to betray you in this room. Yet, I appreciate your apprehension. It will take a brave warrior to accept being tied by bonds he cannot break. As god's father I'm confident that if you're unable to break an enveloping like this -- a silken ribbon, as you call it--then the gods will be awestruck of you and will allow you to travel your individual path."

The wolf lets loose an extended growl. "You All-father, are a deceiver. You breathe in a manner that others don't. I'm not sure you'd let me go when you put me with chains that I could not get out of.

I am sure you'll leave me here. I am convinced that you would like to go and leave me and you betray me. I am not averse to tie the ribbon around my neck."

Odin stated, "Fine language and brave words." "Words to hide the fear that you will be perceived as a coward Fenris Wolf. You don't want to get trapped in this silken ribbon. There's no need for additional explanations."

The wolf smiled as his tongue moved out of his mouth, showing sharp teeth that were the size of the arm of a man. "Rather instead of sneering at my courage I'm challenging you to prove that there is no betrayal is at workings. If one of you places his hands in my mouth, it could tie me. I'll put my teeth gently around the ribbon, but I'm not planning to bite the ribbon. If there's no deceit taking place I'll let my mouth open after I've cleared my mind of the ribbon, or after I've been released and his hand will be safe. That's it. I'll tie you with your ribbon as long as I have my mouth closed I'm going to promise. There you go. "Whose side will it be?" says the narrator.

The gods looked at each other. Balder looked at Thor while Heimdall was looking at Odin and Hoenir was looking at Frey however neither of them moved. Tyr Odin's son was silent and stepped up, extending his left hand.

Tyr told Tyr, "I'm going to put my hand inside your mouth. Fenrir."

Tyr put his right hand into Fenrir's mouth as the way he did before when Fenrir was a pup, and they were playing together. Fenrir shut his eyes and gently closed his mouth until his teeth held Tyr's hand on the wrist, without breaking the skin.

Gleipnir was tied to his fate by the gods. A shimmering path of snails' tracks surrounded the huge wolf, binding his legs together and locking him.

"There," Odin said. "Now, Fenris Wolf, you have to free yourself. Be a shining example to us everyone."

The wolf stretched and squeezed every muscle and nerve in its body to try to tear the ribbon that was bound to it. However, with each effort it seemed that the problem become more difficult and the shiny ribbon became stronger.

The gods first laughed. The gods laughed later. The gods finally laughed when they realized that the beast had been unable to move and they weren't in danger anymore.

Tyr is the sole one to remain still. He was not laughing at all. He felt Fenris Wolf's sharp , toothy teeth on his wrist as well as the dampness and warmness the tongue was feeling against its palms and fingers.

Fenrir put aside his fight. He was in a trance when he lay there. If gods were to release him the moment would be today.

The gods were, however were chuckling even more loudly. Thor's thunderclap laughs were mixed with Odin's dry laughter with Balder's bell-like laugh...

Tyr caught the eye of Fenrir. Tyr looked at him with a fierce glance. Tyr was then silent and closed his eyes. "Do this," he said quietly.

Fenrir took a bite out of Tyr's wrist.

Tyr did not speak. In order to slow the flow of blood into an ooze, he put his left hand on the thumb's left stump, and squeezed it as tight as the he could.

Fenrir was watching while the deities threaded one side of Gleipnir through a massive stone, and then secured it under the ground. Then , he observed as they grabbed another rock and hammered it into the earth at a deeper depth than the depth of the ocean's deepest.

The wolf shouted "Treacherous Odin!" "I would have been a god's companion If you had not deceived me. Your terror, on other hand, deceived you. Father of the Gods, I'll kill you. I'll hold off for the last day of time before eating the moon and the sun. It would bring me the greatest satisfaction to kill you."

The gods were careful not to get close enough to the jaws of Fenrir However, Fenrir turned to snap at them while they pushed the rock further. With a keen eye the god nearest to him sunk its sword through the roof Fenris the mouth of Wolf. The sword's hilt was lodged within the lower jaw of the wolf opening it up and preventing its closing.

The wolf roared incoherently and the wolf's saliva flowed from its mouth. You might have thought it was as a mountain that had an erupting river from an underground mouth if did not know it was an actual Wolf.

The gods left the point where the stream of saliva gushed down the dark lake. they didn't speak until they were sufficiently far away they laughed more, patted one another in the back and smiled the big smiles of people who think they've been smart indeed.

Tyr did not crack a smile or laugh. He wrapped a piece of cloth around his wrist, and walked towards Asgard to meet the gods heeding his own advice.

Then, they were the offspring of Loki.

Chapter 5: Freya's Unique Wedding

Thor the god of thunder and the strongest of the Aesir and the most powerful of the bravest and most courageous warrior, was not yet fully awake however he knew there was something wrong. He reached out his hand to grab his hammer that he carried close to his body at all times, even when he was asleep.

As he closed his eyes the man fumbled around. He searched for his hammer's comfy as well-known shaft.

There isn't any hammer.

Thor opened his eyes. He stood straight. He stepped ahead. He moved about the area.

It was impossible to find a hammer left to be discovered. His hammer had vanished.

Mjollnir is the title given to Thor's Hammer. Brokk and Eitri two dwarfs made it to honor Thor. It was believed to be one among the gods' treasures. The thing would die in the event that Thor hit it with the hammer. If he was to hurl the hammer into something, it wouldn't be missed and remain in his hands after it flew across the sky. The hammer could be slender and hide it in his coat before re-growing it. It was a superb hammer, but there was one aspect: the handle was just a little small, requiring Thor to swing it only one handed.

The hammer shielded Thor and the gods of Asgard from the many dangers that threatened them as well as all the other people in the universe. Thor's hammer frightened the ogres and giants of ice as well as trolls , and monsters of every kind.

Thor was a big fan of his Hammer. The hammer was not to be seen.

If something went wrong, Thor took action. The first thing he did was to ask himself whether Loki was the one to blame for the incident. Thor considered his alternatives. He considered his options. Loki wouldn't have dared to grab his hammer He thought. When something went wrong he did the next sensible step and called Loki to get assistance.

Loki was a businessman with shrewdness. Loki will control his actions.

"Don't tell anyone that the god's hammer is been taken," Thor told Loki.

"That isn't the best news," Loki said, smiling. Let me investigate it and find out what I can learn."

Loki was on his way to Freya's house. Freya was the most beautiful among gods, was also the most beautiful of all. Her golden locks sparkled in the dawn light as it slid over her shoulders. Freya's two cats walked around through the space, eager to aid in the pulling of her horse. The Brings necklace was shining around her neck, shining and golden just like the hair she wore. It was made to Freya by dwarfs who lived deep in.

Loki told Loki, "I'd like to borrow your feathered cloth." "It's it that one which lets one the ability to fly."

"Not," Freya said with a stoic tone. "My most valuable item is my Cloak. The cloak is worth more that gold. I'm not going let you wear it to go about causing trouble."

Loki told Loki, "Thor's hammer has been taken." "I must find it."

Freya told her, "I'll get you the cloak."

Loki took off his feathered coat and flew through the sky in the shape of the falcon. He flew through the skies of Asgard. He floated into the realm of giants, searching for something different from the norm.

Loki was stunned to see a huge grave mound beneath his feet, and the largest, most ugly Ogre the one he'd ever seen was lying on the grave, strumming the dog's collar. The ogre spotted Loki in falcon , he shook his head with a sharp-toothed smile.

"Loki What's the matter regarding the Aesir? What's the latest about the Elves? What's the reason you've gone to the land of the giants on your own?"

Loki is right beside the Ogre. "From Asgard, nothing but bad news. From the Elves only negative news."

"Really?" said the Ogre, who was laughing as if he were elated over everything he'd done and imagining himself to be amazing intelligent. This kind of chuckle was a common occurrence for Loki. Loki himself did it at times.

Loki told Loki, "Thor's hammer is missing." "Do you have any information about this?"

He laughed while the ogre massaged his armpit. He confessed, "I could." "How's Freya?" he demanded. Is she as beautiful as everyone says?"

Loki told Loki, "If you like that kind things."

"Oh yes, I am," the ogre replied. "It's true."

There was a second awkward gap. The ogre threw the collar of the dog into a pile of collars for dogs and began plaiting another.

The ogre said to Loki, "I have Thor's Hammer." "I put it in such a deep beneath the earth that nobody or even Odin will ever be able to find it. I'm the only person who could bring it back once more. And if you give me something you want from me, then I'll give the hammer back to Thor." Loki said, "I can ransom the Hammer." "I will give you amber and gold and I'll give the riches of the universe to you in unimaginable quantities"

"I do not want them," the ogre stated. "I would like to marry Freya," says the Narrator. In eight days bring her here. When Freya's wedding day arrives I'll present the gods' hammer to her as an anniversary gift for my bridesmaids."

Loki was curious, "Who are you?"

The ogre smiled and revealed his teeth that were crooked. "I am Thrym God of Ogres," Loki, the son of Laufey was the reply.

"I am confident that we'll be in a position to come to an agreement and a amazing Thrym," Loki said. The man wrapped his body in the cloak of Freya's feathers and spread his arms and flew off into the sky.

The universe seemed tiny under Loki's gaze: he looked down at the mountains and trees that were as small as toys for children, and the gods' issues appeared to be insignificant too.

Thor was waiting in the god's court and Thor's huge hands grasped Loki before he even made it to the ground. "So What are you thinking? You're in control of every aspect. It's written on your face. Tell me what you're aware of right now. I don't believe Loki. Loki. I'm curious to know what you're up to before you've had the chance to think and plan."

Thor's innocence and rage inspired Loki the one who planned and prepared with the speed at which everyone breathed in and smiled out. "Thrym the lord of all the ogres has stolen your hammer" the ogre stated. "I convinced him to return the hammer back to you, however, he's asking for a price."

"Fair enough" Thor said. "How much?" "Freya's hand in the marriage" says the narrator.

"Is he just after her hand?" Thor hoped. She had two hands, and she might be able to convince her to surrender one hand without difficultly. Tyr, after all, had.

Loki responded, "All of her." "He is looking to get married to the girl," tells the storyteller.

"Oh," Thor exclaimed. "That could cause her to be angry. Of course, you should be informing her about the circumstance. If you're not carrying a hammer you're more adept at convincing people to act than I am."

They returned to Freya's Court together.

Loki told Loki, "Here's your feathered cloak."

"Thank you," Freya said. "Did you find the thief who stole Thor's Hammer?" "Thrym, master of the ogres" tells the narrator.

"I'm very familiar with the man. It's a horrible item. "What is the thing he's looking for from this?" "You," Loki stated. "He would like to marry your." Freya smiled and said a nod.

Thor was impressed by the speed at which she appeared to grasp the idea. "Freya dress in your wedding crown and pack your bags," he advised. "You as well as Loki are headed to the Giants Territory. We'll have to get you married to Thrym in the shortest time possible before he makes a decision. "Give me back my hammer."

Freya was extremely quiet.

The ground, along with the walls were shaking according to what Thor had observed. Freya's cats screamed and mewed and hid in a fur chest and refused to come out.

Freya's hands were tightly clenched into fists. The Brisings necklace fell off her neck and fell to the floor. The woman didn't seem to be aware of anything. She was staring at Thor and Loki as she thought they were the most filthy and most disgusting creatures she'd ever encountered.

When Freya began to speak, Thor felt almost relieved.

She asked softly "What is the kind of individual do you believe I am?" "Do you think I'm foolish?" Is there something that you ought to discard? Do you think I'm the kind one who'd get married to an ogre to keep from getting into trouble? If you think I'm heading to the world of the giants, I'll dress in a bridal veil and crown and submit to your control and manipulation. the lust of this Ogre... the fact that I'd love to get married... " The woman was stopped. The walls rattled once more and Thor worried that the entire structure could fall over on the top of them.

"Get out," Freya said. "Do you think that I'm a sort women?" "However. "My hammer," Thor declared.

Loki told Loki, "Shut up, Thor." Thor was stopped. The two walked away.

Thor said, "She's beautiful when she's angry." "It's easy to understand why the ogre would like to get married."

"Shut down, Thor," Loki repeated.

In the hall of great size where they held a gathering of all gods. With the exception of Freya who was unable not to depart her house, all gods and goddess was in attendance.

They discussed, debated and debated all day. It was evident the gods wanted claim Mjollnir

But how? Each god and goddess offered suggestions that Loki dismissed.

One god Heimdall The all-seeing god who is watching on the Earth, was silent in the final moments. There is nothing that escapes his attention He also occasionally observes events that are yet to happen in the universe.

"How is it going?" Loki inquired. "How do you feel Heimdall?" says the narrator. "Are your abilities to offer any suggestions?"

Heimdall said, "I do." "However you won't enjoy it."

Thor hit his fist hard into the tables. "It does not matter if we prefer the idea or not" Thor said. "We ourselves are Gods!" exclaims the group. There's nothing we here is going to go through to win back Mjollnir, god's Hammer. Let us know what you think and, If it's a good one, we'll be happy."

"You won't enjoy this," Heimdall predicted. "We'll love it!" exclaimed Thor.

"Well I think we ought to dress Thor to look like a bride," Heimdall suggested. He should put on his Brisings necklace. Make sure to put a bridal crown on him. You can make him appear like an attractive woman by placing his dress in. He should cover his face. We'll force him to wear keys that jingle and dress him in diamonds exactly like women do."

Thor declared, "I don't like it!" "People might think... that's fine at first that I dress in women's clothes. It's far from being possible. It doesn't appeal to me. I would never, under any way, wear wedding veil. Isn't that a notion no one would like? It's a terrible concept, and a terrible concept. I have beard. I'm not able to trim my mustache."

Loki is the son of Laufey Loki, son of Laufey, said "Shut down, Thor." "It's an amazing idea. You'll dress in an elegant veil that covers your face and beard if you aren't sure you want the giants to take over Asgard."

"It is indeed a fantastic plan," Odin the All-High declared. Heimdall You've accomplished an excellent job. It's the sole method to retrieve the hammer. Make Thor in time for his big day Goddesses, Thor."

The goddesses gifted him with clothes. Frigg as well Fulla, Sif, Idunn and others as well as Freya's stepmother Skadi were there to help make his dress. They dressed him in most appropriate attire like an eminent goddess at the wedding. Frigg went to visit Freya then returned wearing the Brisings necklace, which was worn around Thor's neck.

Thor's mother, Sif, hung her keys near his side.

Idunn carried all of her precious stones that she wrapped over Thor in order to let him shine and sparkle in the glow of the candle and also 100 white and red gold rings to wear on Thor's hands.

The veil was draped over his face, only showing his eyes. Var who is the god of wedding, placed an elegant crown over Thor's head. an elegant bridal crown that was high and beautiful, and huge.

Var declared, "I'm not sure about the eyes." "They aren't especially attractive." "I definitely do not want to be," grumbled Thor.

Var was focused at Thor. "I could cover them if I remove this headdress. But Thor has to be in a position to be able to see."

"Do the best you can," Loki advised. "I'll serve as your maidservant and guide you to the world of the giants," he said. Loki transformed his looks and facial expression and was now an attractive young woman serving her. "There you are. "How do I appear?"

Thor whispered something in his ear He was probably good for him that nobody heard it.

Loki and Thor took off in Thor's chariot, Snarler and Grinder the goats who pulled it, leapt up into the air ready to start their journey. The mountains split in half while they moved and the ground below the chariot exploded in fires.

"I am feeling a negative vibe about this." Thor expressed his concern.

Loki as a shape of a girl declared, "Don't talk." "Leave it to me to handle all talk. Do you remember that? If you make a mistake that you don't like, you could ruin everything."

Thor made an emoji sound.

They stopped within the court. Giant, jet-black oxen stood motionless. Each one was as big as an entire structure, with golden-capped horn tips, and a smell of their urine that was aplenty in the courtyard.

"Move it You idiots!" yelled a booming voice from the high chamber. The benches were covered with a new straw! What are you really doing? Grab it and put it on straw instead of allowing it to decay.

Freya The most beautiful creature in the world Njord's daughter is visiting us. She'll be irritated if she encounters anything similar to that."

Thor, disguised as Thor and the servant lady, Loki, walked across an avenue made of fresh straw that ran through the courtyard after leaving their chariot, lowering their skirts to prevent getting through the mud.

A huge woman welcomed them. The woman introduced herself to them as the sister of Thrym. She was able to grab Loki's gorgeous cheek with her fingers, pricking Thor with a nail that was sharp. "Is this the most gorgeous woman in the world?" To me, it's not any way. When she sat down to put on her skirts, she's ankles appeared to be as strong like tiny tree trunks."

"It's an illusion by the sun. "She has the prettiest appearance of gods" she said to Loki's bride without hesitation. "I assure you that you will be stunned by her beauty once her veil falls off. Was she the bride or husband? What was the fate of the wedding dinner? I've struggled to keep her from getting too excited because she's so exuberant."

As they entered the hall to celebrate the wedding celebration the sun was setting.

"What is the likelihood of him insisting on me sitting right next with him?" Thor spoke to Loki in quiet tones.

"You have to sit beside the man." He is sitting there."

Thor said, nervously, "But he might try to put his hand onto my side." Loki said, "I'll rest with you." "I'll explain to him that it's our tradition," she says.

They were seated at the end of the table. Loki was sitting close to him, while Thor was seated on the bench right next to him.

He clapped his hands and a throng of massive servants came in. The servants brought five complete roast oxen, sufficient to feed the massive beasts; twenty whole cooked salmons, with each one is the size of a ten year old boy and hundreds of small plates of cakes and frills meant for ladies.

Five additional serving men accompanied them, each carrying the full mead cask and a barrel that was so massive that it shook with the weight of its contents.

"This dinner is for the beautiful Freya!" exclaimed Thrym who could have added more but Thor was already beginning eating and drinking and it was rude to allow Thrym to talk while the bride was eating.

In the front to Loki and Thor there was a table of sweets for the ladies. Loki took care to pick the tiniest of the pastries. Thor took the rest of the pastries with equal focus, and they disappeared beneath the veil, accompanied by the sound of eating. Others, like Freya who were gazing at the pastry with longing were staring at Freya in disbelief.

Freya however, on the other hand, had recently begun to feed.

Thor took a whole one by himself. He consumed seven whole salmon fillets, and only the bones. When a plate of desserts was handed to him, Thor devoured the cakes and fancy pies on it, making the others hungry. Loki often kicked him on the table, however, Thor did not respond to the punches and continued to eat.

They placed a tap on Loki's shoulder. He replied, "Excuse me." "However, Freya, the gorgeous, just finished her third bottle of mead."

Loki's maiden said, "I'm sure she has."

"It's incredible. I've never witnessed a woman consume as many meals. I've never seen a female consume this much food or drink as much mead."

"There could be a reason," Loki said. Thor breathed in another whole salmon , and then took a skeleton of a salmon from beneath his veil. Then Thor took deep breaths. It was like I was watching a magical show. He was puzzled by the easy answer.

"That equals eight salmon she's eaten," Thrym said.

Loki declared, "Eight days and eight nights!" "She spent all of eight and a half days eating nothing because she was eager to go to the Land of the Giants and be with the man she had just met. The maiden is eating again now since she's within your arms." She changed her gaze towards Thor. "It's great to see that you're still eating My dear!" she exclaimed.

Under the drape, Thor squinted at Loki.

"I ought to kiss her,"" Thrym suggested.

"I would not recommend it. "Not as of yet" Loki replied, however, Thrym was already leaning into him and was making kissing sounds. He took Thor's veil in one hand. Loki's maiden pushed her arm up to hold him back however, it wasn't enough. The couple had already stopped their kissing and then returned, shaken.

Thrym gently hit Loki's maiden's shoulder. "May I have a conversation with You?" he inquired.

"Of Of course!" she adds.

They got up and began walking along the corridor.

They thought aloud "Why Freya's eyes are... frightening?" "It seemed as if they were in flames. They weren't looking at an attractive lady!"

"Of Of course not,"" her Loki like maiden replied quietly. "You would never think that they'd be this way. Thrym hasn't had a rest in the past eight days and nights. She was unable to sleep since she's enthralled by love for you that she wanted to taste the love you have for her. She's overflowing with love for you! This is what her eyeballs are telling you. "A smoldering passion."

"Oh," Thrym exclaimed. "Ah I can see." And with a mouth that was the size of an adult cushion, he smiled and kissed his lips. "All right, then."

The table was re-arranged. The sister of Thrym sat close to Thor and gently tapped Thor's hand using her fingernails. She was telling him, "If you know what's suitable for you, offer me the rings." "All of your beautiful golden rings" says the Narrator. In this castle you'll be an outsider. You'll require someone to watch your movements because you're far away from your home and things can become a mess. You're a plethora of chains. Send me some chains to give as a wedding gift. They're beautiful in all gold and red."

Loki asked, "Isn't it time for the wedding?"

They shouted, "It is!" "Bring the hammer in to bless the bride!" he yelled at the top of his voice. Mjollnir ought to be placed on the lap of Freya I believe. Var The goddess of women and men's vows, honour and consecrate your love."

A group of four gigantics carried Thor's Hammer. The hammer was carried from the deepest part within the hallway. In the dim lighting in the flame, the item sparkled faintly. The two threw it into Thor's lap without difficulty.

"Now," Thrym said. "Now, my love, my dove, my sweetness, let me hear your lovely voice. Let me know that you love me. Tell me you'll marry me. Say that you will promise to me your love in the same manner that females have pledged their vows to their husbands and men have committed themselves to women since the beginning of the age of. "How are you feeling?"

Thor was able to grip his hammer's shaft and held it in a palm covered with gold rings. He calmly kissed the hammer. With his hands, it was comfortable and familiar. He then burst into laughter with a loud, deep laughter.

"What I'm trying to say is that you should not have picked up my Hammer," Thor said thunderously.

He struck Thrym one time with his hammer but it was sufficient. The ogre fell down on the floor covered with straw and didn't get up.

The guests who attended the wedding did not be a victim of Thor's hammer which is the ogres and giants. And even Thrym's daughter was pleasantly surprised by a wedding present she had not expected.

The hall was quiet, Thor exclaimed, "Loki?"

Loki was seen emerging from the table, in his initial form looking out over the destruction. "Well you appear to have solved the issue," he said.

Thor was already taking off his female skirts, letting out an exhale of relief. In a room brimming with dead giants, Thor stood in a hat and nothing else.

"There was no need to worry about it being so bad as I imagined," he exclaimed happily. "I've taken back my axe. I've enjoyed a great dinner. Let's get going."

Chapter 6: What Happened To The Runes

And How Runes Came Into Existence

The next issue to consider what happened to the Runes were actually created. Modern writing systems or alphabets, as we call these, are truly modern inventions that have been in use since the beginning of man, and did not really appear until around about 1700 B.C. Prior to that writing was carried out in a different way than what the way we use it the present day. Most often, it was as pictographs and ideographsthat were used to represent objects and other abstract concepts instead of the sounds are used to pronounce words we speak in our day-to-day lives.

These images have been around for a long time and they're really intricate and fascinating to study. A lot of them have been discovered in the caves and rock carvings of Europe Some consider it to date to as early as 17,000 years in the past. In Sweden and other regions of Scandinavia there are a lot of symbols found on these rock carvings are considered to be pre-runic symbols. Later, they were incorporated into certain writing systems that were considered to be runic. Other symbols that were created during the same time, such as the cross and sun wheel, were not changed into runic letters however, they were still regarded as having a magical meaning.

Naturally, as ancient societies changed and expanded and expanded, trade was able to expand beyond the local community, and the world had to adapt. In the midst of it, these small areas were communicating with each other in commerce, as well as new terms were invented. It was necessary to have an improved system in place. That is what we'll discuss here , too.

The First Alphabet

It is believed that the Egyptian Alphabet is often considered as the first ones of this kind of alphabet in the history of the world, although there could have been other nations that attempted to do the same thing before.

The Egyptians could take their symbols, as well as other images and began making alphabets to make words, much like the one we use today, although there are some distinctions.

While it was different from the methods used by other civilizations in the past this actually helped make the writing system more effective. The pictures could be read by various methods, but the letters weren't help anyone understand the message being sent out. The new system was later evolved and was transformed in to it's current Phoenician alphabet, then standardized. It was so well-known it was adopted by the entire Western world. Many of us, now, have heard of it and know the way it functions.

Transferring to the Greeks

While the Egyptians were the first to get things going but they weren't the only ones doing some work on the alphabet in the early days. Actually it was they Greeks were able take some of the concepts of the Phoenician alphabet and develop several of their own.

Actually, we can get the word"alphabet" from Greeks because of the two first letters in their alphabet.

This particular system of sounds using letters was popularized by people who resided in the region of Italy and allowed it to expand. There were several different systems that were based on the Greek alphabet, which began to expand into other parts of Europe and today we refer to these languages as early by the name of "Old Italic." The spread continued to spread throughout the world of ancient times, all the way up to the region that is now home to the German inhabitants, where then they began to create their own language that was based on this too. It is often referred to in the form of "North Italic" in the present. This is the source of some of the Runes that we will look into in this book.

The Germanic Languages

After that, we can go on towards our next chapter, which is the North Italic alphabet, and how this influenced the runes. This is what we'll explore in this guidebook. The initial version of North Italic that we just looked at was difficult to identify even by the most modern experts, and slowly progressed to the north due to the Germanic tribes. These tribes covered an extensive area that extended all the way to Italy and even towards the region of Scandinavia. As the language spread and reached out to the various peoples, it changed and developed.

Nowadays, we can see that the languages spoken between Italy as well as Norway as well as Scandinavia and the other Germanic regions are quite different. However, they do share some commonalities. There are roots for each in northern regions, and at times the two languages sound very like each other, even if they're not exactly the same.

Somewhere between 300 B.C. between 300 B.C. and the 1st century the belief is that certain parts part of Old Italic we are looking at was synthesized into runic symbols, similar to those on the runes, which we'll talk about in a moment. The reason why this was made was to help us develop a runic alphabet people living in this region could utilize. The alphabet was created to show us the sounds that are in German. German language, but it was not in use until that time. It was the Old Italic and some of the rules which went through the Phoenician alphabet contributed to making this a reality more.

In the end and we are left with the Runes. They share many of the same symbols and ideas that they used at the beginning. it can help us ensure that we can see the way they were a few years ago. It is fascinating to discover how this alphabet is constructed and what it represents to us in today's world.

Elder Futhark Alphabet

We'll go at this in the future however, we must have a brief glance at the essence of what the Elder Futhark is about as it is crucial to what we're doing in this article. The Elder Futhark is one of the oldest of the runic alphabet, and it was the one that was used between the 1st and two centuries A.D. these inscriptions were not utilized as part of the system for writing at the period, but rather they were utilized to create magic symbols in charms and amulets. In the past, runes were used for divination purposes to shape and direct the direction one takes.

The alphabet is comprised of 24 characters within the Elder Futhark. So it's not too difficult to understand. As we work through this process you'll begin to understand how it functions and also learn the meaning of each letter. This is the one that we will spend the bulk of our time with but we'll also explore several other possibilities in the form of alphabets and runes in order to assist us on our way. move forward.

The runes we'll be discussing in this book is based upon this type of alphabet. They're a fantastic alternative to use as they are among the oldest and most well-known kinds of these available, they help us understand the magic and the history associated with the runes in the first. There are other alphabets on the market, but we'll take a look at the 24 symbols associated with this particular alphabet and discover how they are meant to function during certain readings.

It is likely this Elder Futhark alphabet is simple to use and can be understood fairly quickly. It is true that the alphabet is displayed will not appear exactly like the one you use for a daily every day basis English. However, it is easy to learn, as it is organized in three Aettir that have eight letters per. Each one will be focused on the various elements and will help you to better understand the kind of readings you can receive from these also.

The alphabet is an essential aspect of being able to utilize the runes you've got and aiding you in reading the divination that is vital to the whole process. We will spend a period of time looking into the meanings of the symbols that appear on the alphabetic letters in the Elder Futhark alphabet, so we will be able to comprehend how to use it and take a look at some of spreads that go with it so that we are able to find the answer to all of our questions.

Norse Mythology and How This can help us understand the Runes

To fully comprehend the Runes it is necessary to take a look at the mythology that is associated with the Runes. This can help us understand the reason why Runes are so magical and how we can harness this knowledge and make use of the Runes to the extent that can enhance our own supernatural powers.

Who is Odin?

Odin is a major part of the mythology of the Runes Therefore, we should spend some time into and find out more about Odin. Odin is often referred to for being the God of divination, poetry, the arts, and wisdom. Odin is the father of Bor and the giantess, also known as Bestla. Odin was the god of Aesir and also the chief of Asgard and was married to the goddess named Frigg. He also is the godfather of many gods we can be able to recognize from contemporary films like Vali, Hodr, and Thor.

A lot of people who believe in this mythology believe that Odin as the all-father. He is often accompanied by two ravens in his midst, as well as two wolves. They accompany him to combat, where the eight-legged horse follows him. One of the ways that Odin can be identified is the fact that Odin has only one eye. He sacrificed it for him to drink water from the Well of Urd. The result was an abundance of knowledge and it is believed that he can have all the knowledge about the universe.

Odin set out to prove himself to be the most powerful and most intelligent god. He was willing to take on any job that could help him achieve this goal but many of the task was lengthy and risky. He took a drink from Urd's Well of Urd, and as we'll discover that he endured many hours of discomfort and suffering to collect the Runes and harness them for his powers as well.

What is Yggdrasil?

To understand the myth better it is also necessary to study Yggdrasil.

The world tree is also often referred to as"the world tree" in Norse mythology. It is the ash giant that is the foundation for all universes. There are nine ways that the tree could assist us in reaching other planets, too. There are three root systems in the tree. The different root types include:

"To the Underworld" (known as Helheim or simply Hel)

* To Jotunheim or the Land of the giants

* The place to the gods and goddesses in Asgard.

These are only three of the worlds we can see in this tree. The others include Midgard, Muspelheim, Vanaheim, Niflheim, Alfheim and Svartalfheim.

At the bottom the walls were of three types which were crucial in addition. The three walls were:

* Urdarbrunnr. This is also known by"the" Wall of Fate. The Fates or the Norns in the

mythology, will be the ones responsible to water the tree frequently.

* Hvergelmir * Hvergelmir wall that is known by the name of Roaring Kettle. The monster known as Nidhogg resided there, and they often would gnaw at the tree's roots whenever they wanted to.

* Mimisburnnr This is the wall that is known as Mimir's Well. it is considered to be being the fountain of knowledge. Odin gave up his eyes in order to get wisdom from these waters.

As well as being a symbol of life, it's an emblem of the interconnectedness with all the things of the universe, and is clearly a reference to travel, particularly spiritual and spiritual. It is the tree whose fruit bring eternal youth to gods, which is the reason it's referred to as the tree that breathes.

There is a belief that when Ragnarok occurs and is considered to be known as the Doomsday according to Norse mythology The world tree, even though it is damaged and altered it would also provide the new, helping restore people and to ensure that the world can return to normal also. According to Norse mythology the world will be over with Ragnarok fight between gods which will take everyone to the grave, with the exception of one man and one woman who, huddled in the hollow of the tree will save themselves from death and bring back life for the entire world.

This tree will provide a little of the background with Odin as he comes to learn of the Runes. Odin was famous for his quest to find water from the Well to acquire more knowledge In the mythology, we'll learn that he also wanted to pursue the Runes to ensure to gain more power than he already had.

The Legend of Runes Discovery

In Norse legends, Odin impaled his heart with his own spear, and was hung from the world tree that was known as Yggdrasil for nine whole days and nights to discover the significance of these runes , which we utilize in the present. The runes were symbolic symbols that came from the source of destiny which was the Well of Urd, and the Norns were then able to use the runes to guide this fate along the trunk of Yggdrasil to locate the nine worlds hidden in the branches of the tree.

Odin was the person who took on this risk and took on a lot of danger and suffering as he understood the significance of what runes were and how they could be a powerful source of significance. He also believed that if he could make it through this test and completely comprehend the meaning and all associated with the runes and gain a lot of strength and insight.

This allows us to understand more of the way that Vikings saw these runes. Although we might be tempted to think of them as a way to convey a message however, they are thought to be more mysterious or metaphysical in nature. The Norse and Germanic peoples were writing using these Runes as early as the 1st century. However, they didn't write using the same style of writing that we use today. They didn't do it in the same manner that other nearby cultures, like that of Mediterranean did.

They were used only for inscribed words that held a large importance. They could be carved into any or all of Rune stones to honor the ancestors , or to signify the graves of people who were believed to be heroes. Because the runes had an inherent meaning they were believed to be a useful way to communicate between the world of the earth and in the realm of the supernatural and, often, they were utilized in spells that promised security or luck.

Without the magical bonds that are associated with runes, and the conviction of the strength and power that are attributed to Odin's quest to have these runes as well There are some interesting aspects of this alphabet , too. for instance it's come in to assist us in identifying your own English letters. For instance, T, F, and S are all parts of runes and we all recognize these as being part of our own language, too.

If we cast these runes whether they're drawn out on other objects such as stones or sticks We can decode the runes and learn some information that could be hidden by other methods. This helps us know what's happening in the present and help us to predict the future much more easily. Instead of being written on parchment or vellum they were often written on bone, stone or even wood. This helped to create a more mysterious style and also ensured that they would be ready to be a part of our lives.

It is believed, from various sources available, that the majority of Vikings had at a minimum a basic ability to read runes which showed the importance of these runes at the time, they weren't just used as an instrument to communicate and read like the alphabet we use nowadays. In fact, many of this time believed that reading the runes, and a thorough understanding of the significance behind them were a way to worship gods and create an impression on the world.

The Tradition and the Magic Behind It

We have had the chance to take an overview of the mystical aspects associated with the runes, it's time to dive deeper into this and discover what it actually is. After we've observed how the symbols that are known as runes evolved into a system of writing that was utilized for several years and centuries, it's time to explore the ways we can utilize the runes of to our advantage today. Although some might like to just collect and use them due to their historical significance, in many times, the best method to make them visible and really get to know the runes from the past, is to incorporate them into our own modern-day divination and magic.

When we read this guidebook, we'll explore how we can make use of these runes, and even make our own divinations through the process. We will also explore the fundamentals to working using this particular type of magic, such as how to create the runes we have created, ways to harness the power which they carry through our spellwork as well as the best way to get messages from the world of the supernatural. This is all achievable and can help us to see the way in which the magic and the tradition of these runes can emerge to play.

Before we can move on with this and truly understand how we can utilize the runes in order to achieve great results using our own magic abilities, it is important to examine the way in that the information in the pages to follow will be linked in as clear of way as it is possible to runemasters who have been around who were in previous times. If you can establish this connection, that's the time to make the most of the runes.

For starters, we need to examine the essence of magic in the present day. A lot of the modern magic we think about today is a blend of pan-European influences. A lot of the ceremonial magic of Hermeticism, Neoplatonism as well as other elements will be brought together to create what is known as the Western Mystery Tradition that we are familiar with today. The best part about this is that it's been constructed with a wide range of folklore and other elements to ensure that there are truly unique magical systems and those who practice it will discover a variety of choices to aid them.

The sources that have fueled the various blends of modern magic were developed can be found from many different locations. For instance, we can see these blends in the oldest texts from Egypt Grimoires from the classical period, and many more. They can be discovered through divine intervention by the person who wishes to utilize the technique.

The magical equipment and supplies used in this practice will differ significantly and at times those who practice magic may include other things such as ritual wants, crystals and plants, pins and bottles and various other things. The truth is that a lot of the magic we are learning about today isn't as simple as we'd like and is mostly due to the fact that it's an amalgamation of many various practices with no precise roots or even ones that can be traced to a particular region in the world.

If we compare modern Western magic which will be an enormous mess that is difficult to follow throughout the process, with Rune Magic, we will notice significant distinction. It is evident when you attempt it and are interested, you'll be sufficiently piqued to give an examination too. Comparatively to what we discussed before the people who use the runes' magic will take advantage of the specifics known about the magical practices that were a part of Germanic people prior to when Christianity was introduced.

This is a great thing. Your magic traditions come from the same people who first had runes and handed them down over the centuries. You can trace your magical history all the way through the ages, and it's not a mix of various items that should remain in place. The runes that have been used for centuries have stood the tests of time and those who use them know the way they function and how to utilize them , too.

The majority of the information about the magic you are about to learn will be derived from a range of literature, lore, and mythology from ancient Scandinavia However, the clues could be found in fragments of mythology that were all over in the Germanic world. We must remember this: it was the case that Germanic globe was far larger than modern-day Germany and that means there were a variety of groups of cultures and people to consider. This can lead to some differences in what we see , but can ensure that we get fascinating insights when working on this.

Alongside the aspects that we have discussed before we'll also see several ancestors that are associated with these magical runes are discovered in ancient texts as well as archeological discoveries and other endeavors that can help us complete the task.

Of course, there's no evidence over the years to build a precise image of what this type of magic derived from runes was about during the time of. It would be interesting to understand the exact process by which they were created and what we can expect to extract from them and more if we were naturally-occurring users of this. This is where we will discover that intuition is a factor in to the process too. Even in the modern day method of doing this, you'll have to incorporate some elements of magic as well as traditions, and your own sense of intuition , too.

However, the level of being able synthesize and borrow practices and beliefs from different traditions, like what we find in the popular magic, isn't as commonplace for people who use the runes. It is possible that this is something other magic traditions can be able to work with. But it's not something that runses will concentrate on traditional methods instead of embracing all the popular options , like the other. This allows us to stay with the more traditional practices and will ensure that we're more likely to adhere to the customs that were associated from the beginning. That could be beneficial. We are aware that these runes have an enduring connection to the history of the Germanic regions.

It doesn't mean that runes only people who use Germanic magic can make use of. If you don't possess the background but you are still able to jump into this area and experience positive results. The energy of these symbols are universal, and they're available to be harnessed by anyone who they're willing to study. It doesn't matter what individual spiritual path or what your religious beliefs are all about.

It can be exciting for those looking to give it a go and are interested. It doesn't matter if you're familiar in a particular religion or have an experience that is different that those from the Germanic region. It's still something that you can study about and appreciate. All you have to do is read through this guidebook as well as other aspects of learning to work with runes in order to achieve this.

The magical works we'll be discussing in this article are designed to be accessible for those who aren't necessarily acquainted with the mythology and spirituality of these particular civilizations. If you're interested in these, you'll be able to discover more about these , and gain a better understanding of the meanings we associate in the runes, however it's not necessary to know about the runes. You will discover that the runes and their stories will help us understand the authenticity of what they are.

The runes are an excellent method of learning more about the beliefs that are prevalent in the Germanic region, as well as some of the practices that are considered magical. If you've been curious about learning the basics of magic and the underlying principles behind that, then the following can be an excellent beginning point for you to get this accomplished. It's not always easy to comprehend, and often it requires all of your abilities and knowledge to master. Knowing a little bit about this traditions and the magic that was created by those in the past can help ensure that you're ready to create a kind of magic that's true and authentic all the way.

Chapter 7: The Elder Futhark

It is now time to dive deep into some of the runes as well as the letters. When we get throughout this chapter, we'll examine the different words , and give a talk on some of them to better know what's going on and how runes work. First, we have to dig deeper at the elder Futhark, and how it is supposed to function.

In the majority of cases when we talk about the runes we could be referring to one or more runic alphabets or scripts which we know in the present. In contrast to our personal English alphabet, there's no single or common collection of letters that could be used as the common runic alphabet.

The reason is because people from the Germanic region continued to expand and migrate into new areas, both in the central and western regions of Europe. While they were doing this their language began to change. They mixed with different cultures that were surrounding them, while others

152

simply changed with the course of time. When these dialects began to differentiate themselves from the original versions that was used, then the original runic script, that we call The Elder Futhark today, was adjusted to meet the requirements of the various languages, which were rapidly changing.

In the midst of all the different runic scripts they were used to represent the new sounds that were introduced into the languages. The old sounds were portrayed using new symbols. Later, there were runes that were completely removed and never used. The whole thing was based on what the area desired to achieve and what sat to the most current needs at the time.

It's not clear what the precise number of scripts written in runic were found in the lands of these peoples and it is possible that there were many. It was a region that covered a large area in Europe and considering the variety of kinds of cultures and the amount of time passed and on, it is not surprise to discover many choices available. This is why you can find two distinctive descendents of the first Elder Futhark that came into large use in the region in the period between 5th century and 12th century.

There was a time when the Anglo-Saxon Futhorc has been the first version that was created in the area that is now Denmark along with parts of northern Germany and spread throughout the world and finally settled in the vicinity of England in the course of time as numerous Germanic tribes moved up to England. However there was Futhark the Younger Futhark that came to replace the Elder alternative we talked about in the region of Scandinavia during the 8th century. It was the script employed during the times during the time of the Vikings.

It isn't unusual to find Neopagan magicians or other practitioners who work with the Runes use particular runes that are from one system by itself However, there are others that blend several, based on their particular style of work. A lot of people also felt it was helpful to integrate some scripts of the runes that were not widely known such as the Medieval or Gothic runes as well as those of the Armanen runes, and many more.

Furthermore to those who use witchcraft, there's another set of what's called witch's runes which are modern and in the tradition of the ancient runes. These are not the ones we normally spend our time with. They might be a bit similar to the runes that we discuss in this article, however they don't have any connection to it.

As we can see it is possible to find a variety of options are worth considering when it's time to understand how to work with runes and take advantage of the tradition and magic in the runes. It is sometimes difficult, and you could be worried about how to study all the various possibilities and keep up with the whole thing when it appears almost impossible.

To make it more manageable for novices, we'll be focusing on only one rune in this book. It one is called one called the Elder

Futhark. The Elder Futhark is considered to be the root of the runes. They are the ones most readily available when you buy an already-made set and you'll find them to be the one you're most likely to meet alongside other practitioners too. You are able to go back to try other scripts if you'd prefer later however, this will help make certain that everyone is on the same page.

The Elder Futhark was given this name because of the initial six runes that comprise the script. It is comprised of 24 symbols and each will represent sounds that is a sound in Proto-Germanic language too. However, a closer examination of the design and the structures that are associated with the script will allow us discover some of the mysteries that go with these runes. They are in the same way they've always been before they were transformed into the written script we know it today.

We'll go over each of them as we go however, this type of provide an impression of what they appear like when they are placed on the stones or any other material that you are looking at. They're different from the patterns and symbols we see nowadays, but it gives them a bit of the ancient traditions that you're seeking within your job.

One thing you will be able to observe about them is their significance they carry. We'll look at several more in the future however Gebo (which represents the symbol with an X) is an offering, and lightning bolts are the symbol for Sowilo which is the Sun. This makes it enjoyable to discover about. In contrast, the names of the letters are found in the majority of the other alphabets founded in Europe do not have any significance in any way. Two exceptions are made to this, which include Hebrew and the old alphabet of Ireland called Ogham. Both were utilized for esoteric reasons.

Names of runes be derived from the everyday experiences of the people who were working with them. Things like horses, trees torches, cattle, and trees are commonplace to be found in our everyday lives as well as they were found within the runes. Then, we'll discover natural phenomena such as solar radiation, frozen ice and water. Intangible experiences are also available as well, and they could include possibilities such as need, joy, and power, in addition to divine forces that could include gods like Ing as well as Tyr.

There are many items that are contained in these runes. This is the reason that makes them distinctive at first. It is possible to look through and discover the meanings and the meanings they represent in just taking our runes and examining the signs. You might even be stunned by an interest in them on the route.

Literal and Meanings Symbolic

We also need to keep in mind that these names aren't always literal when applied to divination or one other types of magic they are commonly used for. In most cases the meanings associated with the runes are likely to include a variety of esoteric meanings and metaphors in the process. Here is an example of this. The illustration of Ehwaz (or horse) is unlikely to be referring to a real horse when used to divinate. It could be a symbol of the virtues of loyalty and trust, an aspect of the relationship between the person riding and the horse requires. It could also be a reference to movement or travel.

It is also possible to look at Dagaz as a word that is supposed to mean dawn. Dagaz is not just about the timing of the day, but often is a symbol of breath-through change, or healing. And often it's all about the possibility of hope. This is why each of the runes could act as an interlude that connects the brain of humanity being and the spiritual world of divine wisdom which the runes are meant to be a part of. When we take a look at not only the symbol but also the meanings that are contained in the name of the symbol We can discover more about the spiritual energies that reside in the runes.

We'll be exploring the meaning behind these symbols as we go However, it was a great way to introduce us to some of the symbols and show us that there is more to the story than we think at the beginning. This is part of the appeal. All of it can be understood by our own sense and the events in our lives right now.

Grups of elder Futhark

Another aspect to keep in mind is the fact that Elder Futhark has been divided into three groups. Each group are able to use eight runes. We'll examine each one of them in more depth in the next few chapters however it is crucial to be aware of them too. They are all referred to as an Aettir and. It refers to an Old Norse word for families and it is a way for us keep track of what they are about to do.

Origins behind this group are not clear, and numerous artifacts with inscribed inscriptions from the complete Elder Futhark represent the runes in a row that is horizontally, not having three rows of 8. Other inscriptions may indicate it is divided in this manner. It could be a way to allow some people to be able to master it quicker than they did in the past however it could be something we have done in modern times, too.

The Aettir or families are named after a god that was the source of the first rune of that particular row. In our one row, we see symbols of Fehu and it's also known as The Freyr's Aett or Frey's Aett. Then , we get the second row that is said to contain symbols of Hagalaz and is Hagal's Aett (sometimes known as Heimdall's Aett). We can then conclude with the Tyr's aett comprised within the 3rd row. It begins by displaying the sign of Tiwaz.

The divisions in these sets make it easy for us to understand and to remember the various patterns that appear in our runes. However, they also help us create patterns of relationship between runes we can utilize to create magical effects in the event that we want to do. For instance, we can also examine the relationship between the two runes in each set to aid us in this regard.

This will comprise the symbolisms associated with Uruz, Nauthiz, and Berkana and we will concentrate on what each is about. The Uruz is about being strong and powerful as well as Nauthiz is all about strength and desire. Then

161

we can conclude by referring to Berkana that is the rune of birth that is both literal on the level of birthing, as well as a metaphorical sense of something that is occurring to you.

Anyone who has experience with the birth process, for instance you know that it takes an abundance of strength needed to successfully deliver a child However, this may often be a sign of the need to give birth to the birth of an innovative idea that gives immense strength to an organization or a plan, for instance, the relationships that are created between these runes and the particular situation that the person who reads these runes has experienced in their lives, will assist you in understanding them with a greater understanding.

It is also possible to consider the fact that many of the mystical students of runes also discovered that each family will have their own specific associations and in relation to the meanings that are associated with each of the runes. The meanings of these runes will differ between different traditions dependent on the specifics you're studying however, we can define them in this way:

* The Freyr's aett will symbolise one of the powers that are associated from the creation process.

Hagal's Aett will be more worried about the potential disruptive forces and changes that may manifest themselves,

*Ty's Aett will close this out by presenting a representation of the divine forces in relation to human interactions.

In order to further expand this The progressive order of the runes as well as how we use them will play a significant role when we read the runes. The reason for this is that the runes within each row are seen as having an inter-symbolic connection to the runes that are placed before or after them. The order in which the runes are arranged will have an impact on the interpretations you obtain.

This adds the complexity of the whole process, which can make it more difficult to master for those who are new. We will however examine some of the readings you can perform to make sure that we fully comprehend the underlying meaning, and we will be able to study some runes, and perform some divinations if we want to when we're finished. As we gain more experience and dedicate more time to the runes, you'll be more likely to being able to understand the meaning of these runes , based on the place they fit into all this.

In some ways the runes could help to find some resemblance to the system of symbology in the Tarot. They're completely different concepts however it's fascinating to consider them in the process. This will help us understand that when we take out these runes, like pulling out Tarot cards The order we choose to use is equally important depending on what its symbol tells us. Due to the similarity of these theories There are those believers who claim that Tarot cards were influenced at least partially however, the runes are not.

Elder Futhark Elder Futhark is one of the oldest and the most original out of the many scripts found within the Runes. This is the reason it is usually the one people spend the most time studying, learning about and deciphering what they can get from the pictures and symbols. Learning about the various Aettir associated with it will allow it to more effective for your personal requirements. We'll go into the subject a little more in the remaining chapters to allow you to complete a few yourself readings.

Multiple versions of the identical Runes

As we've learned in the previous chapters, a variety of other alphabets of the runic alphabet developed following Elder Futhark. But, it's also evident that certain letters of the alphabet are reoccurring in various shapes, as you see in the image below. The most well-known instances include Ingwaz and Sowilo that are equally common in both forms, however too Uruz and Hagalaz aren't often used in both variants of the image.

165

The reasons may not be obvious to us, however they're not too difficult to determine. In the first place, we need to consider the fact that Norse people traveled extensively in the past. And when they arrived in the new location they would often join the culture of the people living there and were in some way influenced by the local culture. A dialect or slang emerged that resulted in slight changes in the way that they wrote. Additionally each Runemaster was distinct in his style, and it's not hard to imagine to see how some in the course of time made a decision to add their own design to the engravings in order to alter some letters.

In some letters it's all about ease of use for instance, Uruz's second form Uruz which was designed to be engraved more quickly and simpler. In other instances it could be because the reasons are more complex, such as Ingwaz which is now the shape of a square, and is believed to make it a less complicated and more harmonious symbol, representing eternality, as it creates an unending and eternal pathway.

However, these letters are extremely old and therefore, we aren't certain about these theories however, we can be confident in being confident that should we come across alternatives to Ingwaz, Sowilo, Uruz or Hagalaz They are similar to the principal symbols.

Freyr's Aett

It is now time to look into the type of Aett which is found inside our Futhark of the Elders. It is known as Freyr's Aett (called as Frey's Aett). It is the runes that provide the necessary information for us to exist on this Earth as well as for being in contact with other people and also with God, and to live the life that is enjoyable and fulfilled. This is an enormous task however it can be quite enjoyable to study. Let's take a look and discover some more of the symbols.

Fehu

First, the symbol that is referred to as Fehu. The most commonly used method to understand Fehu is to think of wealth, specifically about the ability to move wealth. In the time of the ancient people of the present having cattle could be the distinction between being happy and content, as opposed to living in a state of poverty. The animals could not only be something was traded in exchange for other things that were valuable however, they could be able to provide the food you needed as the owner. This could be beneficial in times of need.

Modern versions of Fehu will be more focused on credit and money, because the majority of us do not own livestock that we keep. Credit and money are modern-day versions of movable wealth. But, we could examine a wider significance of the rune that concerns the abundance and prosperity of life in general and other aspects of this , which aren't financial, like lots of food, health as well as the social advantages, or even affection. This is the reason why the Fehu symbol could be a great reminder that we should be grateful for all the wonderful things that happen to us regardless of whether we're not wealthy.

Based on the way you interpret this, and which spread you are using (we will discuss it in a moment), Fehu may also represent good luck for example, more money or a way to combine your wealth. Success in business and other kinds of reward for your efforts can be seen these days. But, it is also important to emphasize that you should share the good fortune you have earned to others, be it within your own family or the community.

When we speak of Fehu It is crucial to stay clear of greed or any selfish behavior to maintain a good relations with those in our lives.

The line to Fehu in the rune of Anglo-Saxon poem says:

Wealth can be a source of comfort to all people

But a lot of it every man will give away

If glory he desires

To make a profit from his god

Fehu reversed can be a kind of the reverse here. It could indicate an eroding of self-esteem, wealth or property. Whatever reason is to be found, the wind of luck aren't blowing your direction right now. Perhaps there's a sense of frustration or disappointment brewing in your life, or perhaps you don't feel like your plans are going according to plan. Sometimes, regrouping is what you need to do by attempting to be more realistic by cutting back on expenses and taking care of yourself and setting a budget. It doesn't mean you're in financial trouble in any way, but it could be an indication that you're required to alter some of your habits.

Keywords to be remembered by using this symbol:

* Beginnings

* Social success

* Healthful

* Reward

* Abundance

* Prosperity

* Wealth

Uruz

The other symbol we could look at is called Uruz. Contrary to the cow symbol we encountered in our first choice, this one is more focused on the aurochs. It is an ox that was wild and fierce of Europe in the past. The aurochs was a beast who was loved by many because of its strength, power and power, however, since they're not controlled this could be a reason enough to exercise prudently, based on the circumstance.

The raw strength and power will be in this symbol. Physical strength is a sign of strength however, emotional and spiritual strength are typically in the spotlight with this symbol. If you're currently faced with a variety of obstacles and difficulties, then Uruz reminds you that you can actually endure this, or perhaps the ability to defend yourself against enemies. If you're pursuing your own goals like this rune may indicate that you have enough energy in your direction to see it come to fruition. Recall the connection you have to your inner spiritual energy and be confident to receive direction to channel your own energy towards a positive result and more.

Another important message from this is that we have to be mindful of allowing our uncontrolled and unfiltered energy to dictate our reactions to any circumstance or utilize this power to control other people. The problem that's offered by Uruz is to control the forces of nature within us all and ensure that we don't utilize this energy to harm others and harm, but instead to serve all of us.

It is possible to reverse Uruz also. If such a situation occurs, it suggests that we did not take advantage of opportunities or did not realize some of the opportunities that were provided to be successful. There is also the possibility of a lack of willpower or motivation and this can be a result from or be the cause of why you feel that you are not moving forward. You might need to think about how you can do to re-energize your self or eliminate the obstacle which is hindering you.

Keywords to be remembered using this symbol:

* Force of creativity

* Endurance

* Energy

* Power

* Health

* Strength

Chapter 8: What The Runes Can Be Used To

Help With Magic And Divination

Becoming familiar with the various Types of Runes

It is essential to learn as many runes as you can, and also to get an understanding with them prior to. This is a good method to ensure that when you are doing the spread, you'll be able to take the time to learn about your own sense of intuition, rather than figuring out the meaning of each rune. The good thing is that re-reading the information from the last few chapters, as well as trying out some of your own readings isn't only enjoyable, but also a good method to ensure that you know the runes you already know.

The runes symbolize a range of elements, both tangible and the intangible, of the universe as we perceive it as human beings. When we add an element of magic it is possible to explore this entire concept and reduce it to a higher level. The symbols of the runes represents an elemental force, or energy, that the person working on the rune will be able to tune to, and are able to use that rune in various ways.

This is where the intuition is a factor. We discussed a number of different meanings present in the runes and they're all similar, yet may be confusing. Sometimes, the reason you are reading, as well as the context, can help you understand what the runes are referring to. In other instances, you might be required to listen to your own inner voice and figure out the best way to discover what is the best path to take in this situation.

The energy that is contained in these runes can be used to communicate some kind of instruction which are magical and designed to be manifested as well as receive messages sent through the realm of spirituality. When we view the issue from this perspective they are easy to use and it's easy enough to identify the kind of rune that is speaking to you, and then to practice and understand how to work using them to create the magic you desire.

The most interesting thing with the runes that you can use is they create a whole spectrum of possible magical outcomes. Based on the time you make use of them, what your gut suggests, and the context for your readingis, the spiritual significance of the runes may be altered each time you use them.

As we said before it's not necessary to have a solid background in the field of magic from Germany or ancient Norse mythology, however any knowledge you acquire in these areas can be helpful. At a minimum having a brief overview of these myths as we discussed in the beginning of this book, will aid in making at the very least some connections to these symbols , and may assist.

It isn't important how many times you read books and discover about the Runes; it is impossible to substitute for actual experience and performing some of these readings using the Runes. This is the best method to get familiarity with them, and to know what each one is about.

You should give yourself time to work on these runes, particularly if you're trying to get a better understanding of the meanings and names associated with the runes. One method you could consider is to research and contemplate only one rune each day. It is only 24 runes, which makes this a great method to gain knowledge about many runes in just a month. It is also possible to reduce the amount of knowledge going through your head at the same time, which guarantees that you'll be able to comprehend the way it functions and why and not be distracted by the other 24 runes available.

It is also possible to take the rune you are required to know to use that day, and keep it in your purse or on the side of you. When you have the chance, pull the rune out and examine at it. You can even keep it by your bed when you're asleep. This will enable you keep it in your mind throughout the day, making it easy to remember it in the course of your day.

When you are beginning to learn about the significance associated with these runes, as well as some divination meanings that may be revealed in your research, be sure not to be too literal and also follow your gut feeling and intuition, too. The intellectual understanding of the rune can be a good place to begin, however you are able to easily alter any information related to the rune if you have an intuition telling you that the meaning is other than what you think it is. This is another realm that is trying to draw your attention on what is true and what's not in your personal experience.

If you're conducting an analysis and discover that you're stuck or does not work as you believe you should, just look at the symbol and pay attention to any emotions or other impressions that appear to be coming through. Certain runes may reveal additional information or appear to communicate with you in a different way than others when you read them. Do not be concerned if you encounter certain runes in a reading which don't wish to speak to you in any way. They will do so at the right moment. Be patient and take what you can gain from every rune even if it's only a tiny amount it will make a huge difference.

As time passes, you'll learn to concentration on the form that is associated with the runes. This will allow you see them more within your surroundings including the cracks in the pavement, in the branches of trees, or even in the clouds when you look at them. You might need to devote longer with certain people than others in order in order to understand the meaning there. Make sure you take your time and choose the approach that is right for you.

The more you play on these runes the more you will be able to tap into the power and magic that's in each. This lets you concentrate on your own magical abilities. The fundamental aspects of this will help you to get started, and you can pay attention to your own inner voice and own intuition, to complete the task and make the most of your studies.

Magic of Speech, Sound and Symbols Magic of Speech, Sound, and Symbol

As we sit here taking an instant take a look at the key aspects of rune symbols and why the language as well as the sound and the symbol are crucial to certain readings you wish to achieve. It may seem like you are making up stories or that nothing is feasible, but with an hour of effort and a thorough understanding that runes are a part of your life, it is possible to learn a lot about yourself and the people you see for these types of readings.

Symbols have played been a component of the diverse mysterious systems we see across the globe. Although we may not consider them this way in our current world however, they aren't simply images. They usually have something magical about them. An excellent method to imagine these symbols while you read is to use them as a means of communicating visually, and not in words, to the universe at any moment.

They are so effective because they allow us to express certain ideas that are complicated, but in a simple way. The process is carried out in a realm that is not visible to reality, allowing us use the skills we didn't know that we had to fulfill our greatest desires. When we find this kind of thing within the Germanic legends, we can see that the symbols of runes were utilized to serve many different purposes prior to being recorded and were incorporated into the core of our language.

It didn't take for long before the runes became part of the writing system which didn't degrade their importance. Actually, it allowed the runes increase their power in a way that was not possible they were before. The reason is due to the fact that Germanic people put an enormous amount of importance on the power of spoken words in comparison to the other methods of communication. Speaking your thoughts loudly was a way to make your thought more real and tangible, and it was impossible to reverse the thought.

That's why a speech that is utterly careless could result in serious consequences, even though you were not intending to harm anyone in the least. It's the same in our world, however we are often tempted to write off the negative aspects of our words by defining the purpose or apologize so that it doesn't be as painful like it did in the old world. The past was a time when if you said a phrase or word, it was in the world regardless of how much you regret the decision later.

The runes were an opportunity to convey our thoughts over distance and over time, especially in a world that didn't have all its citizens proficient in reading, they were powerfulin ways we might not fully grasp in the present. The magical power of the symbol was merged with the full potential that speech can bring, and later connected to that power behind sound which are magical sounds that can be found within the human body. This led to the power of the basic runes we have in the present.

In the present, we frequently find that the rune-workers employ a variety of sources to unleash some potential of the runes. For instance, they could sing, speak and sing names for the ranes in the course of their rituals.

What We Can Do With Runes in our Magical Creations Modern Magic

In this book We've often mentioned the notion that there's a amount of magic from these runes. They can appear quite straightforward. If you do buy one of these runes for your own purposes it is possible that even the more expensive ones are fairly simple with a simple inscribed on them that helps us know what information is on the surface and what symbol are using. It doesn't appear to be a good fit for the realm of magic, however the power of the runes is crucial for our purposes.

Modern magic can be sneered at and some think that it's all fake and isn't real. If you've used these runes and discover the meaning behind them and have had the chance to play with them, these runes could be well worth your time and could be an enjoyable way to master a little modern magic.

People who decide to study the power of runes within the context of the old-fashioned rituals of Germanic people will likely to discover some different perspectives between our own and that of the people living in ancient Northern Europe held all those years ago. Naturally, they will be differences, and both cultures are totally different from each other.